JOURNEY TO HOME

JOURNEY TO HOME

Canadian immigrant and refugee stories of hope and courage

AZHAR LAHER & DAVID GARSON

JOURNEY TO HOME: CANADIAN IMMIGRANT AND REFUGEE STORIES OF HOPE AND COURAGE

Designed by Nhu Vo

ISBN: 978-0-9938242-2-7

Website: **www.ajourneytohome.ca**
Available on Amazon.ca

This book is dedicated to Canada, a nation of Immigrants. These stories exemplify who we are as a people and a country. We honour all those who sacrificed to create this great land and thank them for coming to Canada.

Acknowledgments

This collection of stories have been a labour of love, and each story has given us a new understanding about what it means to be Canadian.

The book would not have been possible without the assistance, support and guidance of so many people. It is difficult to know where to begin giving thanks, but the obvious place to start is with the storytellers. Your tales of hope and courage has made this book possible.

A single email and a brief chat with Renata Dinnoncenzo at Seneca College helped to facilitate multiple discussions about how Seneca could get involved with this project. Renata, your support and enthusiasm for the project is appreciated.

Mark Jones and Kurt Muller have tirelessly supported this project and provided resources. Thank you for your enthusiasm, knowledge, and guidance.

Nhu Vo's (Belle) creative magic has allowed each story to jump off the pages. Your patience, creative ideas and detailed artwork has brought so much meaning to this project.

Thank you David Agnew and Timothy Gianotti for writing the foreword and preface.

Chris Cox—Thank goodness for your editing skills and eye for detail. It has been an immense pleasure working with you.

Keshavaa Shaiskandan and the PEAR team's incredible work with the website development has opened the book to a wider audience. You are the greatest!

We especially want to thank those close to us who were always encouraging and supportive. This project went from a pipe dream, to a possibility, to fruition. Through it all, they never said stop, even when we felt like it. We owe them our gratitude and several expensive dinners...

Azhar and David

Contents

Foreword

David Agnew

I'm honoured to be asked to write the foreword to *Journey to Home: Canadian Immigrant and Refugee Stories of Hope and Courage*, which is an opportunity as well to congratulate Azhar and David for making an important contribution to the legacy of Canadian newcomers.

As president of Seneca, I have the privilege of a front row seat to literally thousands of Canadian immigration stories as our graduates move from their successfully completed studies to building a new life in this country.

What a privilege for me, but what a privilege for all Canadians that these (mostly) young people choose Canada. In every sense of the word, we are a richer nation because of the presence of millions of immigrants and refugees over the decades.

Seneca has many other wonderful immigrant and refugee stories, from our diverse faculty to our dynamic Social Service Worker—Immigrant and Refugee program to our extensive English classes that have helped thousands of newcomers become more comfortable reading, writing and speaking in their new homeland.

With the exception of Indigenous peoples, on whose land we are guests, many of us have an immigrant story. Mine goes back several generations. Depending on which branch of the family tree you climb, you will find a mix of Irish and Scottish farmers, labourers and merchants coming to Canada, in the immemorable phrase, to find a better life.

It has not been, nor is it still, a perfect journey for all. Canada has shameful chapters in our immigration story: the Chinese head tax, the Komagata Maru, the St. Louis and, sadly, too many more. And today, disproportionately, newcomers can continue to face steep economic and social challenges.

As this is being written, Canada has seen a recent surge in racist attacks on Muslims. The pandemic spawned ugly incidents against Asian Canadians. No matter how small a minority is responsible for these overt displays of discrimination, to turn the phrase around, one is too many.

Encouragingly, there is a newfound focus on equity, diversity and inclusion efforts across the country that is going beyond symbols and rhetoric to action and results. There is a particularly strong momentum among young people who embrace the notion of building a future that is truly equitable for all.

And thankfully, there is a broad consensus across the political spectrum that Canada needs immigrants, and Canada continues to welcome tens of thousands of newcomers every year.

But Canada's future is inextricably linked to how well we welcome those newcomers, and ensure they are able to fully participate in and contribute to our economy and society. That is a story that we all can be part of, and make sure it has an enduringly positive ending.

DAVID AGNEW ***became Seneca's fifth president in 2009. He has held leadership positions in public, private and non-profit sectors, including as Secretary to the Cabinet in the Ontario Government, Principal Secretary to the Premier and President/CEO of UNICEF Canada. Mr. Agnew also serves on numerous boards and committees.***

Preface

Dr. Timothy Gianotti

Journey to Home presents a rich tapestry of diverse immigration experiences –from the very young to the mature, from desperate flights from danger or economic hardship to marriage-based migration or professional moves– and traces Canadian stories coming from many continents and walks of life to one ultimate destination. While tinged with a love and deep appreciation for Canada, these stories explore many of the hardships and difficulties immigrants face when coming to Canada: coping with the high cost of living and working multiple jobs at the expense of personal well-being and family time, having one's professional credentials dismissed and being forced to work in more mundane and lower paying jobs until one can win Canadian certification and experience in a chosen field, struggling with the somewhat cold and closed social environment when one first arrives and desperately needs friends and allies within the wider society, feeling the need to work harder than non-immigrant Canadians in order to be valued and recognized as worthy, and feeling socially isolated until one is able to be culturally conversant and fully functional in English, to name a few. These hardships are, of course, all in addition to the occasional stories of trauma that immigrants experience in their countries of origin and/or their journey to Canada and the inescapable sense of dislocation that they frequently feel after arriving in Canada. While none of these stories drills very deeply into the existential conflict and dichotomization that immigrants often feel (see Daryush Shayegan's Cultural Schizophrenia or Persian-Canadian food writer Naz Deravian's essay on her last meal in Iran, for example), they do offer intimate insight into individual struggles to harmonize one's cultural origins and identity with one's new life in a Canadian context. All celebrate the Canadian value of multiculturalism as well as the comparative safety of Canadian society when compared with many other countries across the globe.

Some might find fault with the fact that there are few references here to explicit experiences of racism, even though we must admit that such experiences exist. That said, there is great value in these stories as they are here presented. Indeed, as we continue to grieve and process the recent hate-inspired murder of a Muslim Pakistani Canadian family in London, Ontario, these stories become more and more important for all Canadians to read and ponder. This is because they all speak to the courage, rich experience, resilience, hope, strength, and wisdom that immigrants bring to Canada and also because they remind us that, with the single exception of the Indigenous Peoples of Canada, we are all immigrants whose stories started somewhere else. These stories thus encourage us all to tread lightly, walk humbly, and work diligently to reweave the tapestry of our nation with dignity and respect for all.

TIMOTHY J. GIANOTTI ***is a Canadian immigrant, president of the American Islamic College and Director & Principal Teacher of the Islamic Institute for Spiritual Formation.***

Introduction

Azhar Laher

You can spend a lifetime looking for a sense of home. Sometimes we must leave our home to find it.

In his poem "Journey Home," Rabindranath Tagore writes, "The traveler has to knock at every alien door to come to his own."Home can be a place we belong, home can be found among people we love, home can be carried with you wherever you go. Home is a direction we are tilted towards. Home is something we must remake again and again.

During the American Revolution, slaves from African colonies found refuge in Canada. At the turn of the 20th century, Jews fleeing Russia settled in Canada. In the 1960s, laws were changed to allow army deserters and citizens opposed to participating in the Vietnam War to come to Canada. In the 1970s, Canada welcomed a group of Tibetan refugees, among the first non-European refugees to relocate to Canada. In the same decade, Canada welcomed thousands of Vietnamese and Ugandan refugees. And, more recently, Canada has welcomed over 40,000 refugees from war-torn Syria.

Canada's immigration record is not perfect. In the late 19th century, a Chinese head tax was enacted to restrict immigrant Chinese labour and to exclude immigration based on ethnic background. In 1910, black Oklahoma farmers were denied entry into Canada; in 1914 immigrants traveling from India to Vancouver on the SS Komagata Maru, were sent back to India. Until the end of World War II, many Jewish refugees were denied entry into Canada, some forced to return to areas of Europe still under the Nazi regime. We cannot forget about the detainment of Japanese Canadians in the 1940s. While these are only a few instances, Canada's immigration history shows us that while we

Furthermore, Canada continues to grapple with serious mistreatment and human rights violations of Indigenous peoples and violence against Indigenous women and girls. Canada has a lot of work to do regarding anti-black and anti-indigenous racism and around protecting minority and disadvantaged groups.

It takes courage to leave a familiar place for an unfamiliar and new country. A kind of courage that immigrants and refugees demonstrate every day.

Canada is a country that has welcomed people seeking asylum or fleeing war. However, the majority of people who have made Canada their home have done so voluntarily, bringing with them their knowledge, skills, tenacity and resilience that is so desperately needed to sustain the Canadian economy. Canada is fortunate to attract people with diverse skills from all over the world who want to contribute and make an impact. We are better for it.

By 2040 it is estimated that one in four Canadians will be over the age of 65. Therefore, Canada's reliance on qualified immigrants for its labour force will only increase. The good news, according to Statistics Canada, is that 52% of recent immigrants have a bachelor's degree compared to 24% of the Canadian-born population. The future looks bright for Canada if qualified immigrants are allowed access to jobs that match their skills.

I am an immigrant and I understand how challenging it is to move to a new country. My family's life in Canada would not have happened without the courage of the many immigrants who came before us.

I had lived for thirty-five years in South Africa under a system of legal racial segregation called apartheid or separateness. I witnessed the release of Nelson Mandela, the birth of democracy in 1994 and the anticipation of equality, freedom and peace for all South African's who had suffered for over a century. Our family's move to Canada made me realize that there is no perfect time to do anything. We second-guessed our decision many times and asked ourselves "why should we uproot ourselves and leave our loved ones behind"?

The first few years in a new country increases the number of times you ask that same question. Immigration is not for the faint of heart. You must dig deep every day to make it work. You must be resilient and expect the good with the bad. You must remain optimistic during the darkest days; and there are many dark days in the first few years. To pretend that those dark days do not exist is like pretending that there will be no snow in winter.

Life in Canada is very different from a life in South Africa. The work culture, work ethic and social norms are quite different. I live in Toronto, one of the most multicultural cities in the world, can celebrate how far we have come in being inclusive and welcoming, we must with over 230 different nationalities. Just under remain humble and remember what has happened in the past.

half of the city's population was born abroad. People from every corner of the world come here because we all want the same thing - a better, safer, contented life for ourselves and our children.

No matter how much research you may conduct before arriving as an immigrant, the reality will be different and very uncomfortable when you get here. You must be flexible and comply with new rules, regulations and norms that might ignore your previous history outside of Canada. For example, your work experience may be discounted because it is not "Canadian experience". This naïve, short sighted and siloed notion of work experience must change to attract globally qualified professionals who can see the different colours of the "beach ball". Diversity of thought and diversity of talent is a critical ingredient to remaining competitive in the knowledge economy.

I think about my children two generations from now who will be telling their grandchildren about their Canadian stories. How they conquered the icy storms inside, and outside, of themselves. How they challenged the status quo by bringing creativity and ingenuity to their place of work, and how they returned the favour by making it easier for the next generation of immigrants to succeed.

This is my story.

Perhaps it is your story, too.

Introduction

David Garson

"Give me your tired, your poor,
Your huddled masses yearning to breathe free,
The wretched refuse of your teeming shore.
Send these, the homeless, tempest-tost to me,
I lift my lamp beside the golden door!"

Emma Lazarus wrote these lines as part of her famous sonnet, "The New Colossus" in 1883. These words were so affecting that they were inscribed on a bronze plaque on the pedestal of The Statue of Liberty in 1903.

Lazarus herself was not an immigrant. Indeed, she was from a family with longstanding roots in US soil. She was however Jewish and therefore, at the time, part of a small, maligned minority. She became an activist when she learned about the pogroms against her fellow Jews in Russia. One could argue that she knew they had to find a better way, or more accurately a better PLACE.

Her message also carried a deeper meaning. She put into words what was essentially the reason the USA came into being and why it was growing strong and wealthy. As the old axiom goes...it is a country of Immigrants.

Canada, while not modelling our political system on our southern neighbour did copy them in one very important way. We too were and are a country of immigrants. There have been shameful times in our history when we have turned our backs on this credo, and we were worse for it. However overall, we have been devoted to the concept of immigration as economically necessary and in certain circumstances morally imperative.

Today, we are facing massive challenges to our way of thinking and our conduct as a country and as individuals. There is tremendous pressure on our government to look at the very concept of immigration and its utility.

"May you live in interesting times." Most of us are familiar with this simple statement that is believed to have originated as a curse. At the time of writing this (late 2020), we are all feeling cursed.

There is political upheaval; a deadly and vicious plague; and unprecedented levels of xenophobia, prejudice and intolerance. Even for those that lead what would ordinarily be thought of as privileged lives, existence has become a struggle. Human nature, such as it is tending to look for blame usually finds it somewhere. "Surely this must be someone's fault. I am unemployed, financially precarious and worried. This is no time to let people in who will take more from me."

As a country we have gone through perilous moments ...and we have survived. We are strong that way. In a sense we have learned from our personal challenges. This has been handed down to us by our parents and their parents. It is the immigrant experience: overcoming obstacles to succeed and triumph. It is who we are.

These are the personal experiences of normal men and women who have been faced with many challenges and through determination, will and desire have overcome them to succeed and flourish. The stories are not overly dramatic...just real. Some are similar, others unique, all are interesting.

I have been practicing immigration law for roughly thirty years. I have always told those I work with that a file is more than paper. There are human beings in those pages with fears, hopes and dreams. This book is our attempt to give meaning to those words. As you read through, please give thought to not only what is written but what is meant. You may be surprised at how much you can identify with the people in the stories. I know I was.

Finally, I must mention this: A surprising common denominator in several stories is how much new immigrants could identify with and had empathy for First Nations People. There seemed to be a familiarity as to how some felt they were treated. We did not expect this. There is irony in that those who were here long before us can identify more easily with those that just arrived.

Please enjoy the book.

Design Philosophy

Nhu Vo (Belle)

The design of this book was inspired by the somewhat arduous journey of immigrants and refugees when they leave the land of their birth and immigrate to a new country. The motif that best describes their journey is a maze. Their journeys are fraught with difficulties as if they are travelling through a maze. Their starting point is the metaphorical entrance into the maze and Canada- their destination and new home.

Additionally, to make the stories personal to immigrants and to embrace their origins, I created a series of patterned tiles to depict each of their stories. The patterns and motifs reflect their origins and are indicative of patterns on textiles, floor or wall tiles, and embroidery art from their country of origin.

Details are described below:

Argentina
Inspiration | Argentine traditional textile. The color combination is from their national flag.

Bangladesh
Inspiration | Bangladeshi embroidered quilt called Nakshi kantha. The color combination is from their national flag.

Bosnia and Herzegovina
Inspiration | Bosnian embroidery art called Zmijanje.

Brazil
Inspiration | The decoration tile, azulejos in São Luís, Brazil.

Chile
Inspiration | Chilean traditional textile.

China
Inspiration |The traditional Chinese oriental pattern.

Columbia
Inspiration | Columbian weaving. The color combination is from their national flag.

Holland
Inspiration | Floor tiles. The color combination is from their national flag.

Egypt
Inspiration | The ancient Egyptian lotus ornament.

Ethiopia
Inspiration | Traditional Ethiopian embroidery art in their tunics.

France
Inspiration | Victorian fleur-de-lis motif.

Germany
Inspiration | 14th–15th century German embroider motif from clothing.

Ghana
Inspiration | Ghanaian textile, kente cloth.

Guyana
Inspiration | Guyanese hexagon kites.

India
Inspiration | Indian traditional textile, the sarees and kurtis.

Iran
Inspiration | Traditional Iranian oriental motifs.

Israel
Inspiration | The star from Israeli national flag.

Mexico
Inspiration | Traditional weaving.

Nicaragua
Inspiration | Floor tiles.

Pakistan
Inspiration | Pakistani traditional textile, Sindhi Ajrak.

Poland
Inspiration | Polish folk embroidery.

Romania
Inspiration | Romanian knitted embroidery.

Saudi Arabia
Inspiration | The decoration tile found in Hassan Enany Mosque in Jeddah, Saudi Arabia. The color combination is from their national flag.

South Africa
Inspiration | South African bead art.

Tanzania
Inspiration | Tanzanian textile, Khanga.

Turkey
Inspiration | The decoration tile.

United Kingdom
Inspiration | The British wallpaper.

United States
Inspiration | The star motifs and colors from the USA's national flag.

Uzbekistan
Inspiration | Uzbek embroidery textile, suzani.

Venezuela
Inspiration | Venezuelan weaving.

Hoping to be Complete

Naeem "Nick" Noorani

The story of every immigrant. Something left behind. Something missing. Families, friends and memories left behind. Hoping to be complete.

Photo by Jeanne Menjoulet on flickr

This image by French artist, Bruno Catalan, an immigrant from Morocco, struck a deep chord with me.

I moved with my wife and two children to Canada in 1998. Prior to that, we lived in Muscat-Oman, Abu Dhabi and Dubai and it was not too far from India which was a three-hour flight. This was convenient as I could fly to Bombay in a short time to be with my ageing mother. Also, it was easy to go home for the holidays and spend family time with relatives. We didn't really miss the food from home because in the Middle East any food you wanted was widely available.

When we immigrated to Canada, we quickly realized that the physical, psychological and emotional "holes" became wider. If you wanted to chat with your close friends back home, it was morning for them, and they were at work and vice versa. So those calls became less frequent and eventually were limited to festivals and birthdays until you didn't even notice that they had stopped.

The first death was my paternal grandmother. This hurt because we were very close growing up and we spent lots of time at their home. And, as I pushed memories away the hole became bigger.

By now we had made a group of friends and life went on and we all carried those holes in our chest. This changed after my wife lost her 48-year-old brother a week after we were in India celebrating our wedding anniversary. Now we skirted around those holes and separation, loss and death combined to change us beyond recognition.

My mother had to have knee surgery which was risky as she was keeping poorly, so I went to be with her for the surgery. The flight to see my mother was twenty-four hours. Her surgery was risky, and she was in the ICU. I was grappling with losing a parent. After she was out of danger I had to return to work as the two weeks had already stretched to three weeks and more. My wife flew out to be with my mother and I flew back to Toronto. I will never forget the call I received saying that my mother was no more. There was a gaping wound in my chest that I would spend my life covering. I had now become the man in the sculpture.

I knew I was not the only immigrant to feel this way, and my post on LinkedIn gave others the opportunities to share. That post has had over 84.000 views and 1500 responses.

Here are some of the LinkedIn responses I received in response to the Bruno Catalan sculpture:

I was 16 when I came to Canada some 34 years ago, speaking on migration I often felt this but never was I able to make it tangible till I saw this post! I saw me in this picture and realised that I am still trying to fill in the hole, and make me whole... It's so so true!

Families and friends have to be left behind however memories are always with you, wherever you go.

It is so important that first generation kids in the new land do not take for granted the sacrifice and the great pain and courage that our parents had to make that huge hopeful jump to a new land. I had the honour to take my in-laws and my children back to Halifax and we got to walk those first steps that my in-laws took into Canada. We just stood on those first steps just full of gratitude ... crying an ocean of tears... for all the pain and sacrifice and courage it took and for the Gratitude to where it got them and their children.... I know that my husband and I and so are my kids we are forever grateful.

I remember taking my parents to Pier 21 in Halifax and then the train to Toronto. It was such a beautiful but emotional journey for us all. My dad always said he felt he was always living with one foot in Greece and one in Canada. Not an experience he ever has regretted, but certainly one that has offered many lessons to both my parents, my sister and I, and our children.

'Hoping to be complete' is the essence of the human journey. In migration, there's much to lose and much to gain.

I think we are complete through the new family, friends, and experiences we meet in our new place. We will never be the same, but that's part of the new journey.

When I look at this sculpture as an immigrant, something missing relates to belongingness. People back home recognize you as a visitor and people in the new place recognize you as a foreigner. A classic example of Inclusion on paper versus Inclusion in an immigrant's life.

Oh ...it is so true...very powerful ... I think the majority of newcomers see themselves in this picture, including myself. We left... part of our family is here, another part is there...however, beautiful memories and our roots will be with us forever..everywhere.

Being a Canadian immigrant, I "left" my family behind. My family wanted a better future for me but I never thought it could mean that I no longer could have dinners together with them at the same table.

Mr. Catalano said: 'I have travelled a lot and I left Morocco when I was 12 years old. I felt that a part of me was gone and will never come back. From years of being a sailor, I was always leaving different countries and places each time and it's a process that we all go through.'

NAEEM "NICK" NOORANI

is a social entrepreneur and founder of the Canadian Immigrant Magazine. In 2020, he launched Immigrant Networks helping newcomers create professional networks.

to by Jeanne Menjoulet on flickr

We have the Privilege of Experiencing All Cultures

Latha Sukumar

India

Before I moved to Canada, I was anxious to find a way out of my life of domesticity—to "become" someone. I met my husband in the third and final year of my undergraduate program. My parents wanted to see me married, and he was an eligible bachelor. There was a lot of emotional blackmail involved, so I resigned myself to my fate. I thought, what are the odds I would ever fall in love and marry, given how limited and controlled my interactions with boys were?

I was married a month after my graduation, not quite twenty-one, and soon after left for Malaysia, where my husband worked. Though Malaysia was a tropical paradise, it did not offer any employment opportunities. I was on a dependent visa and homesick, lonely, and frustrated. I put all my energy into becoming a good homemaker since I had little else to do in our tiny village. I knew I was regressing, but I found joy when I had a baby and completed a graduate degree through correspondence.

The opportunity to move to Canada came in 1987. My husband, who had two master's degrees from the U.S., did not mind returning to the West. He moved first, and I followed, a wide-eyed 25-year-old, carrying a chubby and active 18-month-old baby. I had no idea what to expect and was unprepared for what was ahead of me.

We fit the profile of the kind of immigrant Canada was looking for and got our permanent residence in just three months. I was struck by how welcoming people at the Canadian embassy in Singapore were. They seemed eager to approve our application, albeit under the then Prime Minister Brian Mulroney's Conservative government. The government of the day actively encouraged immigration because Canada needed skilled labour to fill its tax coffers.

"I had to trade my Indian clothes for ill-fitting skirts and shoes. I felt barren, stripped of my toe rings, anklets, nose ring, and bangles, all of which did not go with my western clothes."

I received my first job in telemarketing a few days after I landed. I responded to an ad, was asked to read a script in English, and as soon as I had finished reading, I was offered the job. I was ecstatic, but it took me some time to learn the art of making a sale. Even though my English was good, I realized I did not enunciate words with the right emphasis and tone to come across confident. Luckily for me, one of the supervisors took me under his wing and coached me. I was a fast learner and soon became one of their best salespeople. In six months, I was promoted to supervisor.

"The hardest part was remaking my identify."

I had to trade my Indian clothes for ill-fitting skirts and shoes. I was confused as to how I should wear my long hair so as to not look immigrant-like. I felt barren, stripped of my toe rings, anklets, nose ring, and bangles, all of which did not go with my western clothes. Needless to say, I felt out of my element. It took me a long time to become comfortable in my new-found persona and to speak up in public with conviction. It took even longer for people to sit up and take me seriously.

I knew I could not do telemarketing forever. My passion was women's rights and so I wrote a paper on the feminist movement to include with my application to the Master's Program in Women's Studies at York University. To my amazement, I was accepted and embarked on the graduate program with much trepidation. We sent our two and half year old to India to live with her grandparents, since my husband landed a job in his field in Northern Ontario and relocated there. The separation was very hard on all of us, but we had to do this to ensure an enduring career path that would help us make a good living since we had left everything and everyone we knew behind to embark on a new life in Canada.

My professors in the Women's Studies Program encouraged me to speak in the active voice and to own my truth. I felt liberated, and this is what motivated me to study law. I graduated with excellent grades and had the requisite LSAT score to be admitted to Osgoode Hall Law School. Not having gone to school here and knowing very little about the history or politics of Canada, I found the program extremely challenging. However, after a shaky first semester, I finished law school with impressive credentials. I worked every summer and also articled at the Ministry of the Attorney General. However, soon after I was called to the Bar, a conservative government came to power and there was a hiring freeze in government. I did not want to do corporate commercial work. I could have become despondent. But I saw an opportunity. I decided to hang up my shingle in Toronto, while also setting up an office in India. I also took up employment doing grassroots work at MCIS Language Solutions (MCIS) which was the reason I went to law school in the first place. I did not think the job at MCIS would amount to much then. But I stayed at it to make it what I wanted it to be—an organization that impacted the lives of vulnerable people in need. As MCIS grew, I was happily able to give up my sole practice and become its in-house counsel while remaining executive director.

Today, MCIS is a self-sustaining non-profit social enterprise, headquartered in Toronto providing B2B services in 300 languages across Canada. Its 50 different language services include interpreting, translation, dubbing, subtitling, and training. MCIS offers eLearning training programs for those who wish to become interpreters and translators and has collaborations with universities and colleges in Canada and Europe. MCIS has 65 full-time employees, 5000 language professionals and serves 800 customers across all levels of government in Canada and some in the U.S. MCIS builds partnerships with immigrant-serving organizations in communities across Canada and technology partners that provide platforms for the streamlined delivery of its services. Its commitment to recruiting highly qualified newcomers and local language professionals is increasing Canada's visibility as a multilingual hub that can provide language services to the globe.

When I came to Canada, I did not come with any preconceived ideas. The vastness of Canada and lack of family connections provided me lots of opportunities to appreciate silence and introspect. I grew much more spiritual and contemplative and therefore became more secure and a better listener. As I grew more mindful, I reacted less and offered space to people to be more authentic around me. I also began to embrace change easily, looking for the opportunities it brought. More than anything, I stopped trying to live up to an image of how I wish to be perceived and tried to stay genuine and sincere.

Canada has taught me the importance of professionalism, meeting deadlines, being punctual and delivering on promises. It has taught me to articulate evidence-based views in a rational and organized way both while writing and speaking. If we believe that what lies in store is much grander than what we could have possibly imagined, we open ourselves up to all the possibilities.

Canada represents the best of humankind in kindness and compassion. We protect our poor with a social safety net and free healthcare. We have one of the best educational systems in the world, wonderful programming for leisure subsidized by the government, a great library system, student loan programs for post-secondary education, and many adult learning opportunities to study and grow. We respect human rights and have the most progressive laws to support our right to be different. With a refugee determination system that mandates a hearing for all who seek protection from persecution and reasonably progressive immigration laws, we are creating a culturally rich and linguistically diverse society that allows us to experience the world right here. We have the privilege of learning from and experiencing all cultures. Even those who have never left Canada can claim to be global citizens!

Advice to prospective new Canadians

- Have a general vision of what they wish to accomplish in their personal and professional lives.
- Invest time and effort up front into skills or qualifications.
- Set up a routine that includes self-care.
- Stay the course, without being swayed by the flavour of the day, while remaining flexible and adaptive.
- Never give up long-term goals for short-term gains.

LATHA SUKUMAR

is an award-winning lawyer and social entrepreneur who was recognised with the RBC Canadian Women Entrepreneur Award in the Social Change category in 2018. Latha is the Executive Director and General Counsel at MCIS Language Solutions.

We Are Here Because of their Courage

Winnie and Richard Lee

China

My Father Richard and Grandfather Lum Wai are remarkable men. This is their story…

The year was 1955 under the regime of Mao Tse Tung who ruled China with an iron fist whilst the ordinary people all over China were experiencing severe famine and starvation. Working in the rice fields my family could not sustain themselves and often went to bed hungry. In desperation my grandparents decided that Richard, at age 10 and being the oldest of five children, should try and leave China for Hong Kong by any means to earn a living.

In Hong Kong a family friend found Richard a job at a bakery, working 14 hours a day from 11a.m. to 1a.m. He was paid HK$18 a month which is equivalent to approximately $2 Canadian which he sent home to his family in China. This continued for two years. My father tells stories of the times he looked longingly out of the bakery window to see the school children his age walking to school with back packs on their backs. These were hard times and he understood that a young age.

Many people were trying to escape from China. A popular route was to swim the waters, from the coast of China to the coast of Hong Kong. Four times my grandfather tried this. He was caught each time and punished. He tried one more time knowing that if he were caught, this time it would cost him his life. He spent eight hours in the water, dodging Chinese gunboats and battling the tides with his rubber tire. He made it across exhausted but exhilarated to start his new life. Sadly, it was his wife and remaining four children who bore the brunt of the punishment by the Chinese government, something that was never talked about.

"It is our Chinese work ethic, our belief in education, and our strong family values which has allowed us to achieve success."

After spending two years in Hong Kong, my father, Richard, had an opportunity to leave for Fiji where his aunt and uncle lived. He was excited to start school at Grade 5 but soon found that it was very difficult to learn a new language. However, the teachers were extremely patient and kind.

He was impatient because he wanted not only to learn English, but also to earn money, especially when he got the news that the situation in China was very dire.

This gave him incentive to move to Suva, the capital of Fiji, where he found work as an electrician's helper. Now he could earn some money to send to his starving family back in China. By this time, he could speak and write enough English to get by but still had to carry three pocket-sized dictionaries. His superiors saw the potential and offered him the opportunity for an apprenticeship for an electrical engineering program. He struggled for two years because of his English proficiency but by the third year he graduated at the top of his class. Richard then moved to Sigatoka and started his electrical business. He was very successful, getting several contracts for wiring new resorts that were popping up all over the island.

Soon it came time to make a hard decision.

Richard had met Winnie Lee, a Fijian-born Chinese, whose mother, Jang H. Lee, was a widow. She was a strong woman caring for seven children. She had married a wonderful man and father, named Howard Lee, who was fluent in reading and writing English and worked at a wholesale retail store in Sigatoka. Howard's life was short as he contracted pneumonia and was unable to receive proper medical attention. When he died, Jang was destitute. She had choices though: Jang was still an attractive woman and had caught the attention of men who wanted to marry her. The men, however, wanted her to be their wife, but did not want her children. She refused all marriage proposals and decided to raise her children alone. With no social system and a small amount of life insurance, Jang struggled to support the children for many years as a seamstress. She also owned a small convenience store, which brought in a modest income.

"Our family had to work hard to find our place in Canada."

Like all immigrants, Jang encouraged her kids to go to Australia, the U.K. and Canada to start a new life. Soon an opportunity opened for the whole family to move to Canada, as one of Jang's sons had settled in there and was able to sponsor the rest of the family.

Winnie Lee was Richard's fiancé and she had moved to Canada three years earlier. Richard decided to give up his flourishing business in Fiji and immigrate to Canada so they could be together. Interestingly, Sigatoka Electric is a multimillion-dollar business that still operates in Fiji

Richard decided to continue his electrician trade in Canada and settled in Belleville, Ontario. He received his interprovincial license at Algonquin College enabling him to work in any province. Soon after graduation he received a job offer as an electrician at the Canadian National Railway (CN Rail) in Belleville. He was 21 and his colleagues looked at him skeptically, but over time he gained their respect. He was happy to be earning $4.30 an hour. He worked at CN Rail for the next 20 years, eventually moving up into a management position and making a very good living.

He always worked hard, taking on jobs that no one else wanted to do. It is due to these strong Chinese values that we were able to lift ourselves out of poverty to where we are today. From the tender age of 10 years until he was 72 years, Richard supported his mother and his siblings in China—I remember that half his pay cheque was always sent to his "family in China." He never forgot them.

While working a full-time job at CN Rail, Richard found time to operate three laundromats.

While raising three children, Winnie enrolled in accounting courses at Belleville Loyalist College so she could learn how to manage the businesses that they had purchased. It had always been Winnie's dream to get an education—something that was not possible for her in Fiji.

In an era of environmental awareness, Richard had the idea to start a business where he would rebuild starters and alternators. So instead of throwing out and contributing to piles and piles of metal scrap, he learnt how to rebuild starters and alternators. This business is still operating to this day under Lee Starter & Alternators. In Belleville, they raised three children who became university educated and built careers in Canada. We also have six wonderful grandchildren who are thriving in Canada.

Our family had to work hard to find our place in Canada. It is our Chinese work ethic, our belief in education, and our strong family values which has allowed us to achieve success. As an ethnic minority, we had to prove ourselves to gain trust within our communities.

We have made great friends in our communities and our children have grown up to be good people and contributing members of society.

Canada is a peaceful county with freedom some people can only dream of; it is a place where the children can go as far as they want in terms of education, career, and building lives for themselves. Our sacrifices were worth it.

We are very fortunate indeed!

Advice to prospective new Canadians

Immigrants are thought to take away jobs and this has made the immigration process very complicated. As an immigrant, one has to be prepared to be courageous and be able to endure criticism and constant doubts about your qualifications. Creating opportunities for yourself is as important as applying for job opportunities. Strong entrepreneurial skills and the drive to succeed are ingredients for success—don't be afraid to build your network and ask for help. Most importantly, take advantage of every opportunity to gain an education..

WINNIE AND RICHARD LEE

are two proud Chinese Canadians who reside in Belleville, Ontario. They love to cook tradition-al Chinese cuisine and spend time with their grandchildren. They have achieved their dream of giving their families a better life in Canada.

Canadians Can Teach the World About Acceptance

Anonymous
South Africa

I grew up in Johannesburg, South Africa. I travelled by bus to a high school that was 30km away. This was during the apartheid years in South Africa and the school was only for persons of "Indian origin". At school we were not able to choose the courses that were of interest to us. However, we had the most wonderful teachers who taught us well. There were no extracurricular activities to speak of.

I was fortunate to be accepted to the University of Witwatersrand, a university for persons that were white. If you were person of colour one had to get ministerial permission to attend this university. There were probably about one hundred students of colour in the school. Most of those were at the medical school. There were a few in dentistry and a few in engineering.

I decided to become a doctor. During our medical training we were only allowed to see patients of colour. I never interacted with white patients. In light of this, I was not trained or exposed to diseases that appeared in white patients.

I had qualified as a pediatrician in South Africa and wanted to obtain a subspecialty in gastroenterology. I was limited in terms of the countries I could apply to further my studies. I had applied to the Hospital for Sick Children in Toronto, Ontario and unfortunately, my application was rejected. A year later I received a phone call advising me that at the last minute someone had withdrawn from a position, and it was now vacant. I accepted without hesitation as I had three children (two, six, and eight years old) and wanted to further my education and expose my children to a "normal life". The position was for three years. t was a lucky unexpected moment. Canada reached out and chose me!

"We became immersed in a life that was not dictated by the colour of our skin."

I initially came to Canada on a work permit. I wanted to first become a Canadian citizen before returning to South Africa. I had to write many exams to qualify as a pediatrician in Canada.

I moved to Brandon, Manitoba. We spent two wonderful years in Manitoba before we became landed immigrants and were on our way to becoming Canadians. Initially it was rough as we were lonely and experiencing culture shock. I was not earning much at the time and the cost of housing was prohibitive. Maintaining our culture was challenging. For example, finding Halal meat and teaching children about Islam was difficult.

I struggled at work with my first exposure to white patients and families with diseases that

"Canada has enabled me to grow as a person."

occur in the developed world. I also found it challenging to cope with the assertiveness of my peers in the workplace. The patients treated me like a professional but my exposure to racial discrimination had made me over-sensitive.

I think these psychological scars will stay with me for the rest of my life. For instance, my wife and I would go shopping and if there was even a minor conflict with a salesperson, we misunderstood this as racial profiling. In retrospect, I am sure it was not case.

We did not return home mainly because of the rate of violent crime in South Africa.

We enjoyed our first winter as we were exposed to snow for the first time in our lives and I began to enjoy and experience new sports like ice hockey and baseball.

Our social life included mainly interacting with ex-pats from South Africa.

Our overall quality of life had improved. My children could play in a park, which they were not allowed to do in South Africa as parks were for white children only. My children became colour blind, which was very gratifying. We became immersed in a life that was not dictated by the colour of our skin.

The system of apartheid in South Africa had systematically destroyed our self-worth, made us feel inferior and brutalised our psyche. People of colour were expected to perform menial work, while white people worked in offices and in professional settings. In Canada, to our surprise, white people were picking up our garbage. Canadians were polite and accepted us unconditionally. We could go swimming in the local pool and do anything we wanted without fear of being turned away because of the colour of our skin. Living in Manitoba also exposed me to the Indigenous peoples, and I became aware of the appalling conditions with which they lived under. Coming from a country seeped in racism, I could easily identify with their plight.

The last five years have given me much to think about and consider, both good and bad. In South Africa I had a reasonable middle-class life with a good income. I had come to Canada with very little capital. I struggled with the cost of living in view of my salary. For instance, we could only take the children to the cinema maybe once every two to three months.

We missed our family and friends and struggled socially; we were lonely. New births, birthdays, weddings, and graduations were missing from our lives. Death of loved ones far away were the most difficult to digest. Not having closure was painful.

When apartheid came to an end in 1994, I struggled with the guilt of not returning and contributing to the country of my birth.

The guilt has never gone away to this day. Interestingly, even though I was made to feel like an "other" in South Africa, I did not fully appreciate my heritage and culture until I came to Canada.

I was exposed to food and culture from all over the world and appreciated the struggles of refugees from war-torn countries and recognised how fortunate I was despite growing up under the brutal apartheid system. I marvelled at the courage of the boat people, people who did not speak English or French and worked several jobs and professionals who were over qualified for their roles and continued to strive in order to give their children a chance for a better life.

When I speak to friends and relatives about Canada, I tell them about free healthcare, rules and structure and the predictability of everyday life. I also tell them about the positive changes over the 30 years, especially how diverse and multicultural Toronto has become.

I also speak about the injustices done to the Indigenous peoples and how this still has not been addressed correctly.

Canada has enabled me to grow as a person. I have learned to accept people for who they are irrespective of race, religion, ideology, or sexual orientation. I had not been aware that some of the words I used in the past were unintentionally hurtful to people.

I have also changed my views on Islam. There are so many different versions of Islam in Canada and I have accepted this unconditionally. I would be tolerant of people in the past, but I now accept people irrespective of any differences. Canadians, generally, can teach the world about acceptance.

Advice to prospective new Canadians

Immigrating to a new country is not easy. You must be very, very patient. The immigration offices will require details, which you may find silly and annoying, but in the grand scheme that is why the system works.

Like all things in life, there are pros and cons. You will miss family, friends, and special occasions, but you will also discover, learn, and meet new people. Define your "why" and revisit it when you experience challenging times.

Remember, that the beautiful rose has thorns, but the rose is still beautiful. They both exist in the same flower.

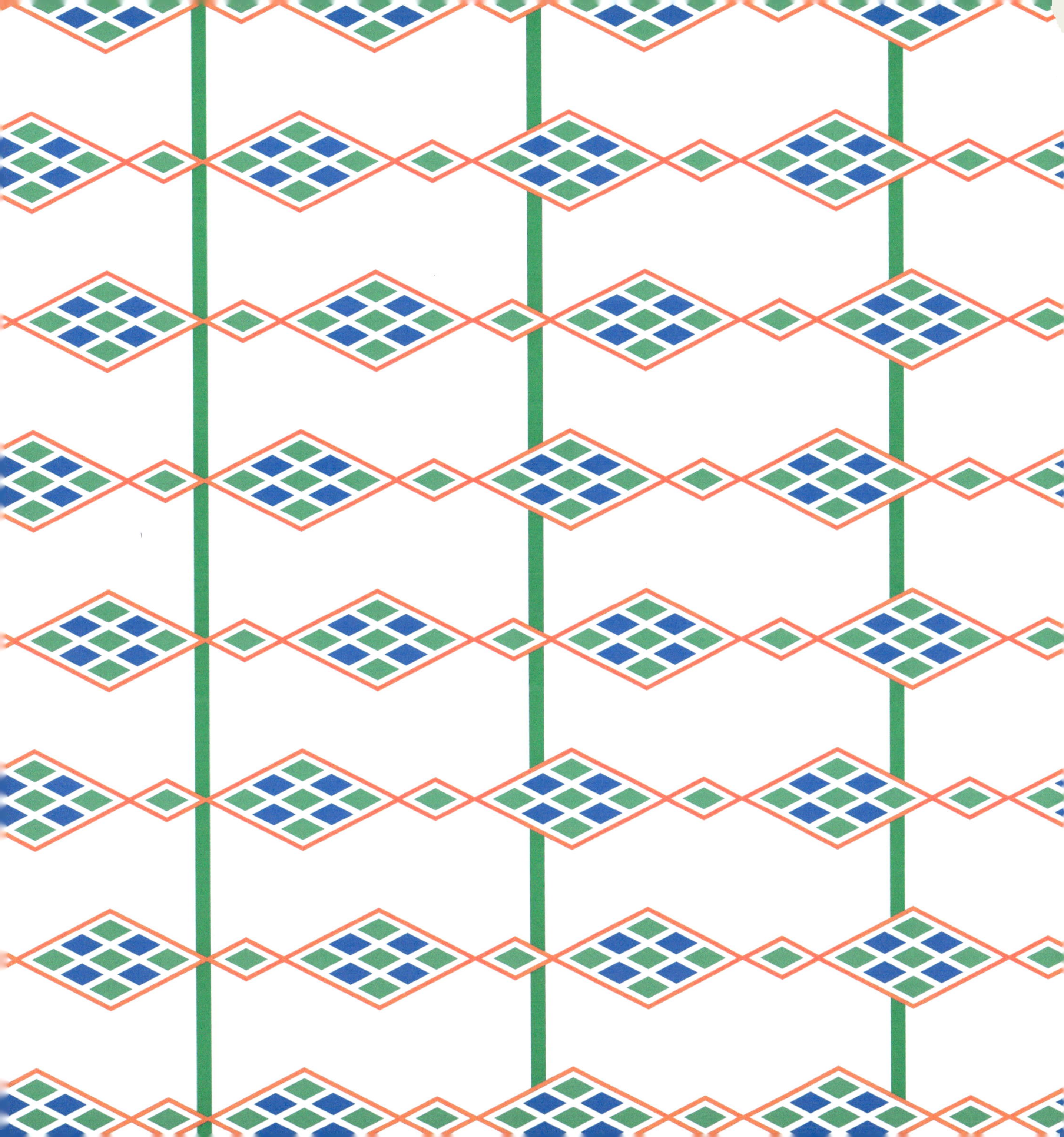

A Realistic View About My Home

Sergio R. Karas

Argentina

I was born in Buenos Aires, Argentina as the only child of my parents, Aria Szmul Karas, a Holocaust Survivor from Poland, and Ana Smoisman Karas, granddaughter of immigrants from Russia and Romania. We were a middle class, but sometimes economically struggling, family. We lived comfortably but without any luxuries. My maternal grandparents often held family gatherings in their small apartment. I attended elementary public school in the morning and Hebrew school in the afternoon. I went to a technical high school and graduated in Chemistry. Life in Argentina at that time was not easy as there was considerable political unrest, terrorist bombings, strikes, and eventually a military coup that ushered a bloody military dictatorship and an economic crisis. We then moved to Canada where I was admitted to York University. I obtained a bachelor's degree in Political Science, and then attended Osgoode Hall Law School for my law degree.

After spending time in Europe and trying to settle there, my father had some distant relatives who encourage him to try Canada. It was somewhat of a haphazard decision, and we fell into it. It was not a deliberately planned move.

We initiated our residency application while we were visitors in Canada. We could remain while the application was in process. As the application was pre-internet days, there was not a lot of information available about how to settle in Canada, so we had to be resourceful and careful at the same time.

"Making friends was the most difficult thing. I found people cold and superficial."

In the first twelve months, getting settled was very difficult. We had no close family and no friends. The worst part was the first winter. We were not used to the extremely low temperatures, snow and ice. We toyed with the idea of leaving. Initially, my father had difficulty finding a job, but he persisted and eventually found one he enjoyed at a major Toronto jewelry store. My parents did not speak English, so they took English classes at night. I worked in a social housing project during my first summer in Canada.

The first five years here had challenges and highlights. To make ends meet, I delivered pizza in the area close to York University during summers and weekends.

Making friends was the most difficult thing. I found people cold and superficial. It took me a while to get invited to parties, for example. I concentrated on my studies, and eventually, things started to change. However, I found Toronto to be very different from the United States. People in Toronto are not as open as Americans. They are ethnically clustered and only socialize with people of their own group. Once I entered law school things improved, as I suddenly became much more marketable in all aspects of life.

Making friends was the toughest challenge, as I did not attend high school in Toronto. Dealing with the winter weather was also a challenge. Perfecting my English to write university-level papers was also a tough proposition.

Interestingly, a friend whom I met during a trip while I was still living in Argentina had major impact on my life before I came here. He gave me good advice. Although we had lost touch for a while, we reconnected by chance after I finished law school and he encouraged me to start my own practice and buy a house.

"Everyone from outside of Canada asks the same question— How cold does it get?"

The answer is not easy. I tell them that we get used to it. We deal with the cold for a few months of the year and try to escape to Florida or the Caribbean for a couple of weeks a year.

After arriving in Canada, I had to learn how to be more reserved. Unlike Americans, Canadians do not appreciate extroverted people, and that is a challenge for anyone coming from Latin America. We are warm, extroverted, a bit loud at times, and a lot of fun. Canadians are very serious, politically correct, and afraid to speak up. They want everyone to conform to the average. It is difficult to stand out, so I had to learn how to blend in without losing my identity.

If I could share the lessons I have learned, I would advise the following:

- Do not expect anyone to give you anything free, you must work hard and carve your own path. I started by delivering pizza in a dangerous neighborhood in Toronto. No one gave me any handouts. I never collected welfare, never expected the government to support me. You should not either.
- Do not come to Canada making demands. Many new immigrants and refugees complain constantly about various aspects of life in Canada. If you do not like Canada, leave. No one is keeping you by force. There are a thousand hard-working people from around the world ready to take your place for a chance to work hard and progress in life.
- As an immigration lawyer, I have observed that some immigrants and refugees look for ways to obtain free services, government support programs, do not make friends outside their ethnic group, and do not participate in activities with co-workers. This is a mistake. You need to integrate into society, not expect society to adapt to you.
- Do not act as a victim, and constantly complain about society's shortcomings, or be envious at the economic success of others. Instead, plan on how you intend to get ahead.

- Be reliable, responsible and dependable, and people will appreciate it.
- Be grateful.

Bono said, "The world needs more Canada". I don't know if I agree. The world needs good people of all nations who can distinguish between right and wrong and act accordingly. Sometimes Canadians think too highly of themselves, believing themselves to be "world saviors" because our politicians have perpetuated that myth. Instead, we should focus on improving our own society, reward hard work, lower taxes to encourage entrepreneurship, and take better care of the elderly. We have enough problems in Canada. We do not need to spend valuable resources in countries governed by dictators and human rights violators who steal our aid.

Advice to prospective new Canadians

If I could make just one point to those who wish to immigrate, it would be that nothing comes without sacrifice and hard work.

SERGIO KARAS

is a lawyer at Karas Immigration Law Professional Corporation, past chair of the Ontario Bar Association Citizenship and Immigration Section and editor of the Global Business Immigration Handbook

I Overcame My Challenges by Challenging them Back

Vanja Lakic

Bosnia & Herzegovina

My parents, older brother, and I fled the Balkan civil war in 1992 when I was five years old to became refugees in Germany. There, my dad, a civil engineer, worked at a recycling plant and later at a construction site. My mom, an accountant, couldn't find a job at all. She found it difficult to learn German and mostly stayed at home. My brother and I were in school. We both made friends quickly and learned German with perfect accents. My parents say they were well received by German families and will always remember their generosity.

When the Balkan War ended about four years later, we had three options: to stay in Germany; go back to Bosnia; or apply for immigration in Canada and Australia. Both my parents were drawn by Canada's promise of economic and political stability. They believed the lives of their children would be better. Thus, they applied for immigration to Canada in the fall of 1995. In 1996, after taking medical exams and interviews, we received a residence permit and arrived in Canada. At that time, I was nine years old, and my brother was 14.

We arrived in Canada with four suitcases in the summer of 1996. My parents' friends had kindly welcomed us into their home for a week allowing us some time to find an apartment in Etobicoke, Ontario. We had come with some money, so our first 12 months weren't as painful as those in Germany. My dad couldn't find a job

"I also became exposed to many more cultures and religions than I had ever been before."

as an engineer right away. At first, he plowed snow, then worked as a machine operator at a factory. We moved from Etobicoke to Scarborough within the first six months. I remember that neither my brother nor I were happy in school during the first year. My brother had left behind a group of friends in Germany, and I was bullied for not knowing English well enough. Not long after, I was named Student of the Month by an English teacher who I admired and who told me that I had a gift for languages. One of my highlights was receiving a writing award. That accomplishment stayed with me for many years to come.

After two years, my dad found a job as a civil engineer in Waterloo, and we moved there. I began to play competitive tennis just like my brother. Our lives focused on tennis practices, tournaments on the weekends, and school. My mom went to English classes and landed jobs that were progressively more in line with her qualifications. We still struggled financially but things were starting to improve. However, my mother developed mental health issues related to separation anxiety from her siblings in Bosnia and my parents' marriage underwent a stressful

"My Canadian experience taught me that soft skills make a difference in the real world."

time. My biggest challenge was learning English while trying to fit in and make friends. I had a healthy distraction of school and tennis to keep me occupied.

Canadians have taught me a great deal. I've adopted a more practical and casual way of life living in Canada. I used to help my mom iron every piece of laundry when we lived in Europe but apparently, nobody ironed laundry in Canada.

"I also became exposed to many more cultures and religions than I had ever been before".

I also learned to adopt a more open-minded view of family structures and relationships. Coming from a nuclear family, I became exposed to children in school whose parents were divorced, kids who had two moms and two dads, stepmoms, and stepdads. I also became exposed to many more cultures and religions than I had ever been before.

I remember that I also felt compelled to smile at strangers which my family wouldn't do coming from Europe—a more coconut society (hard to crack at first but soft inside). I felt at first that Canadians were fake for smiling and engaging in small talk. But I eventually learned to smile more and got better at small talk.

Later, I went on a university tennis scholarship to the United States where I met the most wonderful tennis coach. He selected me first in the lineup in my freshman year where I gained the confidence to lead a team through my example of hard work and a positive attitude. This shaped me as a person. He believed in my ability to perform well on and off the court and gave me the chance to prove that. He named me Sportsman of the Year in 2005 and appointed me team captain in my senior year. He taught me the importance of identifying and working on my weaknesses to become a better player, how to be a feisty competitor and win tight matches, and to think beyond myself because individual victories did not win team championships.

My Canadian experience taught me that soft skills make a difference in the real world. Skills like the ability to advocate for oneself, communicate, network, and influence people. Canada is a land of opportunity where everyone has a chance to succeed in their personal and professional lives.

Looking back, I think that I would have benefited from engaging in social activities in high school to build friendships and leadership skills. I think there is a tendency among immigrant children to aim for high marks and get admitted into top colleges and universities, thus less emphasis is made on soft skills. This could be a reason why immigrants are vastly underrepresented in corporate leadership roles. I certainly wasn't equipped with those soft skills when I began my career as I had been conditioned to think that my professional success would align closely with my strong academic performance. In Canada, I see an opportunity to better understand how non-visible characteristics like speech and socialization can thwart immigrants from achieving their full potential.

Advice to prospective new Canadians

Even though housing costs are high, winters are long and traffic in major city centers is bad, Canada is a land of opportunity with a strong economic and political climate. Everyone has a chance to succeed in their personal and professional lives. Canadians are also open-minded and big-hearted. The country is clean, and most people are concerned about the environment. It is, for the most part, a safe place to express one's individuality. Canada's strong economic and political climate makes it a great place to live, build a career, and raise a family. I believe many countries in the world should emulate Canada.

VANJA LAKIC

is a former NCAA Division 1 tennis player and a graduate of Columbia University's School of Journalism. She has worked in corporate communications, digital media, and public policy.

The Best Decision We Ever Made

Abraham and Ruth Franenberg

Israel

I grew up in Milan, Italy until the age of 18, while my husband Abraham grew up in Wroclaw, Poland until the age of 11. We met in Israel, got married and had our two daughters there.

Life in Israel before coming to Canada was somewhat comfortable although neither one of us had ever fully adjusted to the Israeli mentality (and the extreme heat). I worked as an aesthetician for approximately five years prior to immigrating to Canada and my husband Abraham was a purchasing manager for Israel's largest bank where he was employed for 25 years.

We lived in a very nice neighbourhood in Israel with our two daughters, ages 18 and 12. There was no real immediate reason to leave. However, the national security situation was shaky, and terrorism was on the rise in the late 1980s. Abraham was still not done his mandatory reserve duty in the army, which back then included all male Israeli residents 54 years old and under. There was always the fear of another war. He served in three prior wars and was part of the army for 27 years (three of which were mandatory and 24 as a Reservist).

Fearing for the safety of our family, we wanted to explore our opportunities for a better life for our daughters. Canada and Australia accepted immigrants at the time and the process was simpler than the U.S. And Canada was closer than Australia.

"Life in Canada has allowed us to become more patient, polite, and generous."

A year and a half prior to immigrating, Abraham and I visited the Greater Toronto Area (GTA). We both fell in love with Canada instantly. Our hearts opened during the visit, and we realized the significant differences between the countries—especially the culture and politeness (and the pleasant climate).

During our visit we met with an immigration lawyer and were happy to learn that we were good candidates to qualify and apply for permanent residence, with Abraham being the principal applicant as a skilled worker. We began the process immediately upon our return to Israel. However, in the middle of the process we were notified that the list of professions changed, and Abraham's profession no longer gave us the requisite points. To our surprise, aestheticians became one of the professions in demand and I was then switched to be the principal applicant. From that point the process moved quickly and smoothly. Within a year we received our landed immigrant documents. However, we did not "land in Canada" until six months later as we wanted our daughters to complete the school year without interruptions.

We kept this process confidential until we were approved and ready to leave Israel, mainly due to Abraham's employment and to save us from the unwelcoming opinions and judgment of extended family members and friends. We were so determined that this was exactly the path we wanted to take that we tried not to let anything get in our way.

We became permanent residents in June 1990.

The first 12 months in Canada were very productive. It was a significant adjustment for all of us, as no one really prepares you on how to be alone in a new country speaking a different language and without your family and friends. We both managed to secure jobs, bought a house, and both daughters adapted very well in a short period of time.

It was important for us to live in Thornhill, Ontario where there was a large Jewish community as this allowed us to keep our traditions, meet friends and enjoy familiar Israeli cuisine. While we chose Canada to be our permanent residence, Israel will always have a special place in our hearts. It is a big part of us, our culture, and who we are today.

Within five years of living in Canada I opened my own business as an aesthetic while Abraham entered a business partnership in a computer retail company. Unfortunately, this business failed, and a lot of money was lost. We had some financial challenges at that time but with hard work and determination we bounced back. Around the same time our eldest daughter got married and shortly after Abraham and I became grandparents for the first time—this made our lives very bright. In addition, after three years (and counting), we became Canadian citizens. Taking the Citizenship Oath was a very big day for us. It felt like a huge accomplishment. Throughout our time in Canada, we never applied for or received government assistance of any kind and never felt entitled to anything that we did not earn or achieve on our own.

When speaking with our family and friends outside Canada we always emphasize the inner and mental calmness we feel here in comparison to the uneasiness and daily life stresses of residing in the Middle East. Life in Canada has allowed us to become more patient, polite, and generous.

Canada is a very generous country, always trying to help other countries and still accepting immigrants and refugees. Going through this journey makes my family and I thankful for this country that we are privileged to call home.

Advice to prospective new Canadians

If we can share some life lessons about our journey and give advice to anyone thinking about relocating to Canada, we would encourage individuals to do their research, come prepared with the proper legal immigration documentation, and to keep an open mind with lots of patience. This is a long process that is hard both financially and mentally.

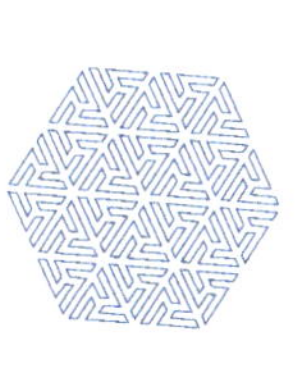

It Is Cold Here, But the People Are Warm

Anonymous

Brazil

I was 21 when I first came to Canada. My years in Brazil until then were very happy and fruitful. I grew up in a suburb city, about one hour away from the capital of Sao Paulo, and lived, not a rich, but a comfortable life with my parents and younger brother. I used to be a professional swimmer in Brazil, winning several championships for long distance freestyle. My highest achievement was to win second place in the Brazilian National Championship for the 800m freestyle. Swimming taught me discipline, concentration, ways to overcome failure and, most importantly, to never give up your dreams. Due to my swimming achievements, I was able to earn scholarships in private schools, which financially helped my parents provide me with a good education all the way through high school.

After graduating from high school, I was accepted at university to study for a bachelor's degree in Science Nutrition. I was 17 then and I continued to compete for my city during my first two years of university. However, I had a very difficult time trying to reconcile my training with my school assignments and exams. I had to train at 4a.m. (for about two hours), then I would go to university (located two hours away from home with traffic), come back home to have lunch and get ready for my afternoon/evening training (this would include gym and about 10km of swimming challenges). I would return home about 9p.m. and begin studying and/or doing homework for school.

"After a few months of living in Toronto, I saw a world of possibilities."

After enduring this very demanding schedule for two years, my body started to give up (I was fainting every week) and my doctor suggested that I choose either my professional swimming career or the completion of my education. I decided to quit swimming when I was at the top of my career. This decision came with mixed feelings. I was sad that I was leaving my team behind (my second family for many years), but I was excited to start a new chapter in my life; one without pressure to have to wake up super early every day. I constantly had to watch my diet and miss fun events with my family or friends because I had to practice during the evening or weekends.

I started to make new friends in university and go to nightclubs and other private parties. I felt like I was finally free and wanted to make up for the fun that I missed due to my swimming career all at once. I never got involved with drugs or abused alcohol (I was never interested in these things probably because of sports), but I started to notice that many young people were, which was very sad. At that time, I was going clubbing at least three times per week and

"I realized how safe I was when walking around the streets in Toronto."

I enjoyed dancing and listening to loud music. My parents were quite concerned about this change in behavior, and, I imagine, they were also concerned that I would get involved in some bad habits. Luckily, I had learned to control some bad influences with swimming and, in the end, all that I wanted to do was to go out and meet new people.

My parents were also concerned for my safety. Sao Paulo is known for being a dangerous city, but I was at the age when I just wanted to be adventurous. I was fortunate that nothing bad ever happened, but I gave my parents many headaches by going out and partying as much as I could. All of this happened in my third year of university, right after I quit swimming. When I started my fourth and last year of university, things became more serious with school, and I had to work in five different co-op opportunities to write my thesis and graduate from my program. I matured a lot during that year and that's when I started to realize that I wanted to switch all that drive I had from swimming to my future career as a dietician. I knew I would be graduating from my school at the end of that academic year, and I also knew that I wanted to specialize in sports nutrition. With that idea in mind, I started to do some research on where to apply for a Master of Education in Sports Nutrition. The admission requirements for any master's program in science always included fluency in the English language, something I didn't have at all. That made me think that I would probably have to go abroad for one year to acquire the language skills I needed in a short period of time.

Since I was very young (graduating from university at age of 20), I was in no rush to start working right after graduation. My parents at that time were going through some family issues with my grandparents (my mom's father had cancer and my mom's mother was in her final stages of Alzheimer's), but even then, they were supportive of my studying abroad for one year. I felt very guilty and selfish for deciding to leave them behind (at a time that they really needed my help), but I was young, ambitious, curious, and ready to see the world. I left Brazil three months after my graduation, leaving behind my family, my friends, and my boyfriend at that time, as well as all the comfort I had living with my parents. It was April 3, 2005, when I first I landed in Toronto, Ontario with a study permit to learn English for one year in a private English language school.

I chose Canada because my father's sister had moved to Canada about five years before. My parents knew that they could only afford to send me abroad with assistance from my aunt for food and accommodation. At that time, I did not expect to stay.

My permanent residence application was a long process. It took me about nine years from the first time I arrived in Canada to obtain my PR status. Since I came to Canada with a study permit, I was not permitted to stay after I had learned English. My parents had agreed that I would only spend one year in Canada and then I would return to Brazil to apply for my master's program. Not only had my parents thought that I would return to Brazil after one year, but also my boyfriend at that time did too. After a few months of living in Toronto, I saw a world of possibilities. I was enchanted with everything I was seeing around me. More importantly, I realized that I could learn about all the different cultures in the world in one place.

Being a girl from a very dangerous city, I realized how safe I was when walking around the streets in Toronto. Having experienced five different robberies during my teen years (with a gun to my head), I suffered from trauma as a result. Feeling free and safe was not a feeling I wanted to go away. I decided not to return to Brazil. I wanted to build a family here and be able to offer this freedom and quality of life to my kids one day. I broke up with my boyfriend and told my parents that I would try and stay in Canada if I could. This is when my journey began! My parents said that I should try to support myself if that was my decision. I guess they

"My first 12 months in Canada were confusing, exciting, and fulfilling all at the same time."

were trying to convince me to return to Brazil. This didn't happen... my fearless persistence and dream to live in a first-world country overcame my fear. One year after being in Canada, I met my husband in a restaurant where I was serving (to help pay for my tuition fees). Five years later we got married. I applied for my sponsorship application. It took almost two very painful years for me to receive a response from Immigration Canada. I was stuck in Canada under implied status for my post-grad work permit and could not leave the country to visit my family. I received my PR status in January 2013, and I remember it being a very emotional day for me. Three years later, 11 years after I first arrived in Canada, I was able to obtain my Canadian citizenship.

My first 12 months in Canada were confusing, exciting, and fulfilling all at the same time. I remember feeling like I was on an emotional roller-coaster. One day I would cry non-stop missing my family and friends. On another day, I would be super happy and amazed to be experiencing such a different lifestyle. Then again, I would be down, frustrated, and ashamed of my language skills.

When I left Brazil, I was considered a popular girl and I had a large group of friends. Coming to Canada, the first thing I noticed was that people tended to be more reserved, and they didn't open up as much as Brazilians did. In Brazil, you would hug and kiss on the cheek when meeting someone new. Here, a handshake is typical to respect others' personal space. I would have to work hard to make friends. It was even more difficult as I could not communicate with them at all (I started my English school in Level 1). I knew that I had only one year to learn English and I tried my best to focus only on the positives while I continued to try to make friends and practice my language skills. I decided to avoid associating with those who spoke Portuguese, and this was the best decision I made. I learned English fast by putting myself into situations where I had no choice but try to express myself, even if it was grammatically wrong. When I learned to not be afraid to speak, things started to open for me a bit more.

It was also very difficult for me to be away from my parents during that first year. This is something that never gets easier. I had to learn how to handle being sick by myself and try my best to stay focused on my goals.

For reasons I can't explain, I feel that coming to Canada completes me. It feels like I was meant to be here. Even though nothing came to me easily here in Canada, things seemed to align very smoothly and there was always a door that opened for me somehow. Even when I have felt blind and frustrated and have had to adjust and be humble enough to accept unexpected changes, I know all will be well.

Initially I was studying English full-time and looking for a part-time job that could help me pay for my expenses. I found a job as a server in a Brazilian restaurant (since I couldn't speak any English yet) and tried to use that experience not to only help me pay for my school but also as an opportunity to practice my language skills. I was studying and working very hard, and I was sleeping only three hours per night. The restaurant I was working at was very far from my relatives' place and I had to commute for about one and a half to two hours for work. I remember that the hardest part was waiting for the bus for a long time. My relatives lived in Vaughan and buses were not very frequent. During the winter, this was extremely painful. My body was not used to the Canadian cold, so it took me a long time to adjust to the new extreme weather.

At my English school, I slowly started to make friends and socialize a bit more. This helped improve my English skills very fast and I began to enjoy my stay in Canada. I went out with my friends and traveled around Ontario to see what this place had to offer. How fascinating and remarkable that experience was! I was feeling alive and hungry to learn new things about all

> **"Everyone who immigrates to a new country will have their ups and downs."**

the different cultures that were around me. I made friends with other international students, and it was always so exciting to hear their stories and share mine with those who were interested in learning about Brazil.

At the same time, being so close to other international students was very unstable because they would come and go, and I knew that I was prepared to stay. I realized that I was ready to start meeting people that lived here instead. My focus changed to meeting Canadian citizens who could teach me how to best appreciate this country and would take me a step higher with my language skills.

At the beginning of 2006, I started working at another restaurant, a Brazilian steakhouse, more upscale than the first restaurant I worked for and more Canadian-oriented. This was the perfect opportunity to achieve a higher level in my language skills. By serving non-Portuguese speakers, I was forced to communicate in English in a more formal way, and to learn more Canadian expressions. A few months later, a very cute guy started to work there too. He had immigrated from Romania when he was 11 years old, and I was excited that he was open to sharing his story with me. I was also happy that I had made a Canadian friend who could correct my language skills without judging me. This was the beginning of a long, and at first complicated, but very happy love story. That "cute guy" is now my husband, and we now have two beautiful sons together.

I accomplished a great deal in my first five years in this country. I became fluent in English within the first year (that was my first goal) and adapted well to the cultural changes. I was able to pay my tuition by working very hard. I had four to six part-time jobs. In 2007, I was accepted into a diploma program at Seneca College. I also won first place in the Selection for Skills Canada competition. I received the Seneca Leadership Award and Outstanding Recreation Council Contribution and made the College President's honour list. My academic career there culminated with being chosen as the valedictorian for my graduating class of 2009. That same year I became engaged and went back to Seneca in 2010 to work as a support staff.

There were many obstacles to overcome including language and cultural barriers, homesickness, weather, changing careers, the immigration process, and having to work while studying full time.

My husband has had the biggest impact on my life. He has been very supportive of me overcoming my language and cultural barriers and has helped me adjust to this new country.

My husband and his family became my second family. Since they had immigrated from Romania in 1995, they were able to share their stories and support me with through challenges I was facing while settling in Canada.

I tell friends and family that Canada is safe, clean, and full of opportunity. Even for those who are unable to successfully achieve all their dreams, Canada is a country that will at least offer quality life and enough support to those that just want to live a normal life. The minimum salary wage can provide the bare minimum to a family. I also usually mention to my family and friends that I appreciate that due to the multicultural city we live in, most people tend not to judge others by appearance. People also respect your space and are very polite and considerate.

The weather in Canada is also a popular topic with my Brazilian family and friends. Coming from a tropical country, it is very unnerving for them to know that I live in a country where winter is so harsh and long. My response to them is that Canada is indeed cold, but we have a structure to support the extreme weather temperatures. Houses and public spaces use heating systems, and the extreme cold weather would only affect you if you were exposed outdoors or if there is a power shortage. One complaint I do have however is that the winter season here is too long for my taste. I miss the colours and the sunshine. Canada is too brown and grey during the winter season. Snow will always be magical and surreal to me, but almost six months of cold weather is too much.

I have noticed that I have adopted some new behaviors since I came here. I check the weather before leaving the house and I find myself talking about the weather with strangers. Brazilians never do that as the weather is one of the things, we don't have a problem with. I do not kiss or hug someone I just met. I now use a handshake. It is interesting that when I go to Brazil to visit my family now as I feel very uncomfortable when strangers try to hug or kiss me. I no longer judge others based on their appearance. In Brazil, for safety reasons, I used to distance myself when I saw someone that dressed in a certain way or had a certain look. I drink water from the tap. In Brazil, you cannot do this. I can consider myself more open-minded. I accept differences and do not judge others based on their ethnicity. I focus mostly on people's attitudes and the way they act.

I tell others in the same situation to never give up or put yourself down because of your lack of language skills. Coming from a third-world country, I made the mistake at the beginning of my journey to think that everyone who had been living in this country longer than me was automatically better. This is not true and, when my confidence returned, I was able to better see my future in Canada and fight for my rights and dreams.

Everyone who immigrates to a new country will have their ups and downs, but if we believe in ourselves and have patience and persistence, things will eventually fall into place. By facing our difficulties fearlessly, we will become stronger and better people. This is the biggest achievement we could ask for and something nobody can take away from us.

Canada is a very welcoming and inclusive country. This is a place where different people and cultures from all over the world come together, without judgment or discrimination. This is what the rest of the world needs the most. At the end, we are all humans with the same needs.

Canadians are also very involved in their communities and care about their environment. People are constantly looking for ways of giving back to society and they work together to keep our country peaceful and clean. Together we are stronger. Therefore, it's very important to be open-minded and put aside all the other differences. The focus is not on trying to change others but on what is best for all of us.

Advice to prospective new Canadians

My advice to prospective immigrants before relocating is to connect with people who have been living in Canada for a while. They can share their stories, experiences, and expectations of the country. This can save you a lot of money and headache. The more research you do before relocating, the easier the transition will be.

Moreover, it is very important that anyone who decides to immigrate to Canada comes with an open mind. Immigrants will have to constantly improvise when things don't happen as planned. It is always good to think in advance and be permissive. It is crucial that you follow your heart and be ready to adjust.

The writer is a proud Canadian who enjoys traditional Canadian pastimes while still maintaining an enthusiasm for Brazilian traditions.

From Chile...to Cold

Pablo Vivanco

Chile

"The challenge for many young immigrants is one of identity and belonging."

I was born in Vina del Mar, Chile, where we lived until I was six. My sister and I lived with my mother after she separated from my father (divorce in Chile was not legal back then), and although we lived in working-class neighborhoods and less than luxurious conditions, my mother was able to afford us a decent standard of living through her work as a microbiologist

Our life in Chile was calm and normal, despite the abnormal situation. Chile was undergoing a deep economic recession under a military dictatorship, but as kids we were pretty unphased, playing in the streets and going to school.

My mother then met my stepfather. Unable to find employment in Chile, plans were set in motion for us to come to Canada (unbeknownst to my sister and I). At the time, Canada had opened its doors to people wanting to leave Chile due to the human rights situation in the country.

My stepfather had been in Canada during the 1970s, working in Edmonton, Alberta and Montreal, Quebec, and some of his brothers had also moved there. To my parents, it seemed like a logical move.

My first twelve months in the country were a blur. I remember my first day at school, learning to say 'hello' instead of 'hola', and learning about the sports that kids played (hockey instead of soccer). My sister and I were the first non-English speaking kids in the school, and as a result, the school began an ESL program.

We moved into a two-bedroom apartment at Weston and Sheppard with my stepfather and his brother. This meant I shared the second room with him, and my older sister slept in the walk-in closet in my parent's room. My parents worked a lot, and my sister and I were busy adjusting, making friends. According to my parents, I was able to acclimatize quickly. It did not take me long to learn the language and integrate. I even enjoyed the winter and the snow and ice, though I'm sure this is true for most kids. My older sister had a harder time, and my parents struggled for years with the language and isolation.

There were highlights in my first five years here. Among the things I remember most were learning to play hockey and skating, visiting Niagara Falls, and of course, our family buying a house. It was at this house that we really began to settle. We set down roots and made friends and connections in the neighborhood that we have maintained to this day. The families on the street exposed me to different cultures and activities such as camping and traveling to other places in Ontario.

The challenges we faced in the first few years were largely around keeping our heads above water while we settled. My parents worked long hours, looking to get overtime to bring much needed extra income into the household. My mother went to college to have her degree validated. It was evident to me, even at that age, that my parents were sacrificing a lot of themselves to keep food on the table and pay the bills. Our family never went hungry, but we also didn't have a lot of time as a family as a result. When we did, our folks were tired and sometimes impatient.

The person who had the biggest impact on my life in Canada was my neighbor, Victor Hugh. Victor was 60-something when we moved next door to him, and he quickly adopted me into his family like a grandchild. I would spend a lot of time at his house, playing cards or watching sports, hearing his stories about his childhood during the depression, union organizing as a tire worker at Goodyear Tire, and many other things. Victor had numerous grandchildren, many of whom were my age, so I was invited on trips with their family and forged close friendships with many people in the family.

As a former factory worker, Victor was a large man, and he defended the immigrant kids on the street against racist abuse from other neighbors.

I tell friends and family at home that there are amazing things about living in Canada, as well as some not so pleasant and frustrating things. I boast about the array of people and foods in a city like Toronto, including the calmness and relative organization of the society (folks from the developing world know what I mean). I speak about the universal programs we enjoy like health and education.

That said, people often ask about the weather. Obviously, I tell them that it is unbearably cold at times. The high cost of living in Toronto often leaves people shocked.

Among the attitudes that I have adopted here is a certain measure of cosmopolitanism—appreciation for diversity of people and cultures. It is plausible that I would have picked this up elsewhere, but the reality of Toronto forces this perspective upon you.

Having now lived outside of Canada for a while, I have also learned to appreciate the value of having public institutions and laws that work and are effective. This includes everything from traffic rules to public transit, to health facilities, and vaccinations.

The challenge facing young immigrants is one of identity and belonging. In this vein, I would say that I appreciate the fact that my parents insisted on maintaining aspects of our culture—including language. It has been important for my career and also for my own development as a person. That said, I have also embraced the hybridization of my own culture with the realities of living in Toronto, including language. As a result, I feel like I have been able to navigate my diasporic identity in my current home as well as in Latin American when I have lived and travelled.

While I acknowledge that living in Canada has been relatively good to me and many others, there are also people in Canada that have not done as well, like the Indigenous peoples. I do not think they need "more Canada". Moreover, Canada has been increasingly vocal in telling other countries how they should operate, and this isn't a positive thing.

Nonetheless, Canada does have many positive policies regarding social inclusion, social programs, and safety nets. Unfortunately, I think that in many ways, it is much harder to move and settle in Canada now than when I came to this country in 1986.

In 2010, I began a sponsorship process for my wife, and it was complicated, expensive, and long. We were separated for more than one year as she had to return to her country to get medical attention that she could not afford in Canada.

Also, major Canadian cities like Toronto and Vancouver, BC are now among the most expensive cities in the world to live in, and this takes a huge personal toll on everybody. Many people must work a few jobs just to make ends meet. Building some financial security becomes more difficult by the day.

"The challenge facing young immigrants is one of identity and belonging."

Advice to prospective new Canadians

Be aware of the good and bad...and bundle up....it gets really cold.

PABLO VIVANCO

is a Chilean-Canadian community worker and journalist. His experiences range from working at Toronto City Hall and North Toronto and serving as director of a media outlet in South America.

I Understood the Language... Not the Culture

Zoe Zhu
China

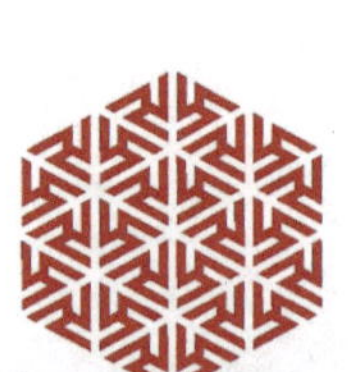

“Life was very good. Why change?”

Before coming to Canada, I was teaching at a reputable university in China. I was an assistant lecturer at the same university, teaching the first- and second-year university students college English. Around that time, the university enrollment in China went up significantly and there was a huge demand for teachers that teach college English. After graduating in 2001, a job was waiting for me. My first two years of full-time teaching was great. As a daughter to a dedicated primary school teacher of over 20 years, going into a classroom to teach was not strange to me at all. The university I worked for provided a small one-bedroom apartment on a low-cost monthly rental agreement to new faculty like myself and I lived on campus. From time to time, I was invited to translate or interpret for some small-sized private organizations, so I was able to earn some extra income. On weekends, I usually spent time with my family and friends, chatting about our life and work. It was fun.

In the early 2000s, the Canadian government opened the door to skilled workers around the globe. In China, many young professionals wanted to go abroad to study, live, and work. After dating for two years, my husband proposed, and we decided to marry. Having worked as an IT engineer for a few years, my husband was confident that he would be able to land a job in Canada. Although his job paid very well, he worked in another city, which was about a two-hour bus ride from where I lived. I remember he asked me if I wanted to immigrate to Canada. I asked him, why Canada? He told me that he had always wanted to go abroad to live and work and that Canada was on his bucket list for immigration. He thought it was a good idea because he had a few friends who also applied to immigrate to Canada. Of course, I didn’t really pay much attention until the day when he told me we had got the immigration visas approved by the Canadian embassy. It was a surprise. I was shocked by the news as I was not prepared at all. We both had good jobs at the time and were surrounded by family and friends.

“Life was very good. Why change?” I kept asking myself. Being the only child, I was very close to my parents, and they had just retired and moved to the city where I worked and lived. I honestly thought that the timing was not good to leave my parents behind.

When I told my parents that I might move to Canada, they asked me if it is for the long term or short term. I said to them that I may immigrate to Canada. They were sad but supportive.

When we received the letter from Immigration Canada, we had about six months’ time to prepare and get things ready before the immigration visas expired. I convinced myself to learn about Canada, and I decided I would apply to a graduate school in Canada. I applied to three universities: York University, University of Toronto, and Queen's University for doctoral studies in Education, where I was rejected from all three due to a lack of academic publications. However, I received the news that York University would accept me into the Master of Education Program. I was so excited and told my husband: "Let's pack up and go!"

My husband and I landed in Toronto on June 28th, 2003. A couple of months before we left China, I found out that I was pregnant. We were excited about becoming new parents with our first baby, but very quickly that excitement was taken over by anxiety. Now looking back, I was proud of myself that I had the courage to leave the comfort of home and come to Canada with a husband and an unborn baby. The first year was very hard for us. We didn't have any family and friends to stay with. We didn't know too much about the city. I remember in the first 10 days after we landed, we lived in a three-bedroom apartment along with two other families from China who were also new to the country. It was a temporary rental apartment for new immigrants; a place we found online through an ad before we left China. These early struggles would end up creating everlasting friendships that we have maintained until today.

Ten days after we landed, we secured a rental for a one-bedroom apartment near the York University campus. Around the same time, my husband started going to English language classes and looking for work. While we waited for our healthcare cards to arrive, we made friends and one friend referred her family physician to us after learning that I was pregnant. My first pregnancy checkup was arranged as soon as I received my health card three months after landing. I was so happy to hear that my baby was doing well and when I saw the ultrasound image of my baby, I was in tears. The school had started in early September, and although I was doing well with my studies, I felt lonely. The colleagues in my programs were mostly full-time teachers at local elementary and high schools and their discussions were mainly based on their observation of what was happening in their classrooms. My teaching experiences were different, and I found it hard to present my thoughts and observations from a different perspective.

My classes usually started at 5p.m. and I spent my days in the graduate lounge writing essays. It was so quiet that I had to talk to myself to feel my own existence. A naturally introverted person, I felt awkward around so many people who didn't share the same background. I remained quiet most of the time and listened to the conversations of fellow students. The topics of the conversation were wide ranging, from TV shows, movies, sport, music to politics and the economy. I was unfamiliar with the topics that were discussed. Before I immigrated to Canada, I had imagined that I would meet with peers and talk about the tv show Friends, which was their favourite TV show. After going to school, I realized that I didn't know any Canadian TV shows and there were many topics I knew nothing about such as hockey, Indigenous peoples, and Black history.

One day, an Asian woman, about the same age as me, entered the lounge and chatted with everyone in the room in perfect Canadian English with no accent. I was very impressed. She told me that she was from China too and had been in Canada for over a year working two part-time jobs and studying full time in the same program as myself. We bonded right away!

I asked her about her thoughts of Canada. I remember her saying, "You just need to enjoy stepping out of your comfort zone and you will like it here." In other words, nobody knew me so I could become whoever I wanted to be. I could see from her face that she was happy. Our friendship had changed my perspective and through her I made a few more friends and we started visiting each other regularly. She also connected me with a professor who hired students as assistants for his research projects.

My due date was in January and as the time got close, I started feeling anxious. As a new parent, I attended a prenatal class learning how to stay well and healthy during the pregnancy. It was difficult for me to walk long distances as I got closer to my due date. We didn't have a car at the time, so I stopped going out grocery shopping. My husband usually walked to the grocery store in the snow and carried home fresh produce and meat in a big backpack.

"You just need to enjoy stepping out of your comfort zone and you will like it here."

Winter came and we found ourselves unprepared for the wind chill and the mountains of snow. I had hoped that my parents could visit us before the winter, but since we didn't have jobs, it was impossible to get visas for them. In the middle of November, I received a package of baby clothes and blankets from my mom, and I sobbed when I opened the package.

My mom knew it was hard for us. A few days after the New Year started, my baby girl was born. I remember her beautiful face. It was like a miracle! My anxiety had evaporated in the months that we had to learn to become new parents. Taking care of a newborn was harder than we thought. Sleep deprivation made us feel exhausted all day long and I felt guilty whenever I had to leave her to attend school. I was worried all the time about my baby's health as she wasn't gaining as much weight as she was supposed to. The doctor kept telling me that I should feed her more, but it was easier said than done. In addition, my husband's job hunt was not successful, and he was not happy. In the spring, we decided to purchase a car. Life was a lot easier after we had a car. I was offered an research assistant position with professor at York University. With the money I was able to cover our monthly rent and utilities. My baby finally started increasing her appetite and she had her first growth spurt when she was about four months old. This was our first year of life in Canada: despite difficulties, loneliness, tears, and anxiety, we also grew, celebrated, and accomplished much.

Five years after we landed in the GTA, my husband and I found jobs that were relevant to our fields of learning. We both started building our professional and personal networks. We had bought our first townhouse and became Canadian citizens. My mom came to visit us twice and she helped us take care of my baby girl so we could focus on our careers. In 2006, I applied to sponsor my parents. Life was getting better every year. In the summer of 2008, I was pregnant with my second child. Compared to the first pregnancy, this one was so much easier, happier and I was more prepared. We bought lots of baby stuff during the pregnancy and my workplace even planned a surprise baby shower for me. I felt blessed that we were able to overcome the challenges and started enjoying life.

I think the biggest impact on my life in Canada was learning to become a parent. Before I moved to Canada, I was in my mid-20s, living on campus. I did not have to take care of anyone: when I was hungry, I would simply go to the student cafeteria to eat. Now I am in my mid-40s, taking care of three children and supporting my parents, who immigrated to Canada a few years ago. My husband and I learned how to cook, how to understand the Canadian education system, and navigate the overall Canadian work and community culture. We learned to celebrate different holidays like Halloween, Thanksgiving, and Christmas, and we explored different foods. I learned how to ski along with my kids and now I can enjoy the cold winter more than before. Raising three children has also forced me to be involved in the community.

I tell people that Canada is a beautiful country with much to explore. There are new cultures, languages, food, activities, ideas, perspectives, and so on. You will be able to enjoy life in Canada if you are determined to explore and prepared to experience something new.

While living in Canada, I have adopted the following new behaviors, attitudes, and perspectives:

- Always keep an open mind. Canada is diverse; learn to appreciate the many cultures.
- Enjoy your life by stepping out of your comfort zone.
- DIY: Do It Yourself. Labour is expensive.
- Speak up and tell people what you think and how you feel.

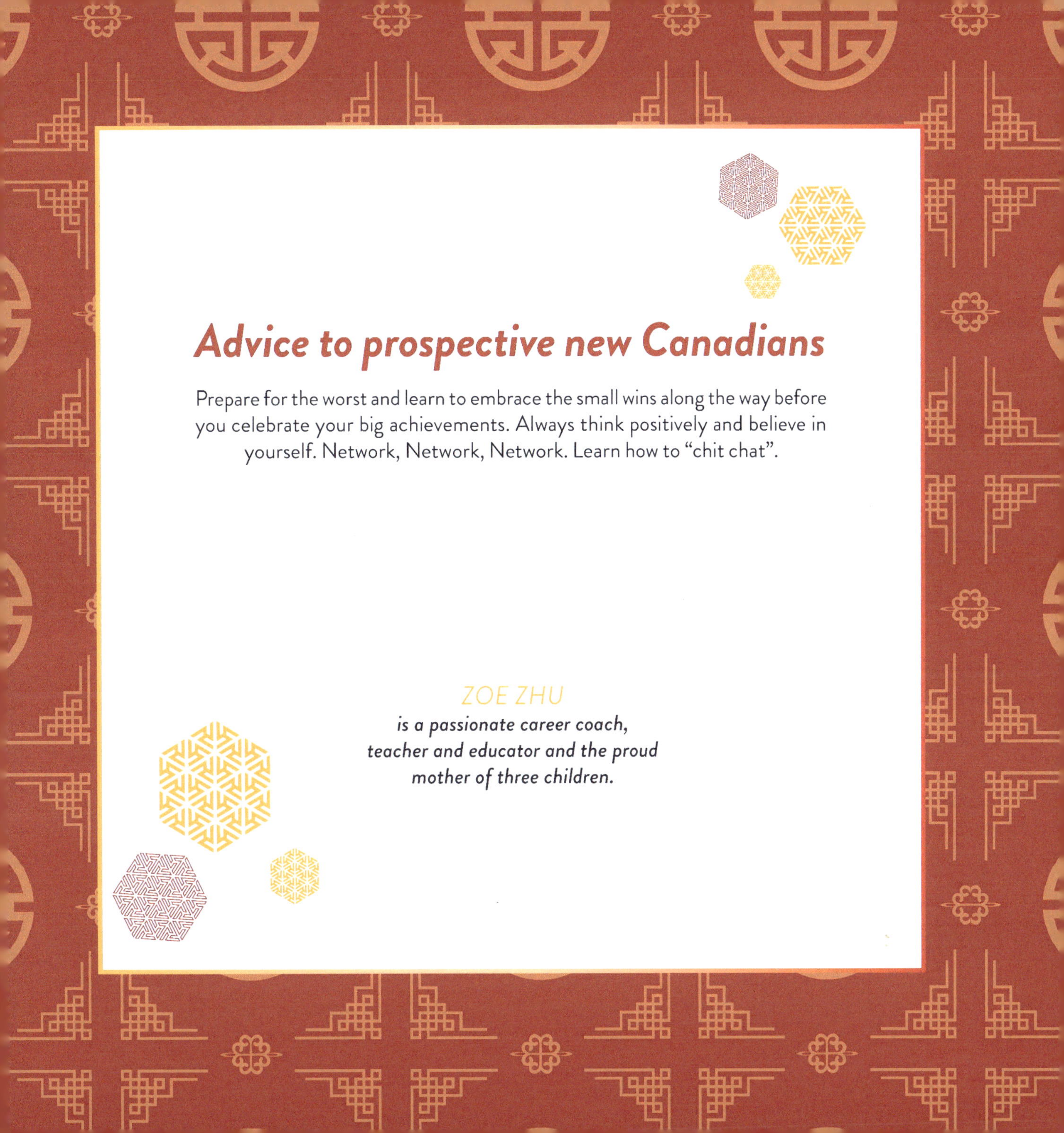

Advice to prospective new Canadians

Prepare for the worst and learn to embrace the small wins along the way before you celebrate your big achievements. Always think positively and believe in yourself. Network, Network, Network. Learn how to "chit chat".

ZOE ZHU

is a passionate career coach, teacher and educator and the proud mother of three children.

Dedication Will Always Prevail

Mauricio Ospina

Columbia

> ***"Everything that happens in the world can be either an opportunity or a threat."***

In the late 1980s my family lost everything due to the country's economic difficulties and civil war related to narco-traffic and guerrillas. My family was middle class and I had four siblings.

My maternal family stepped in to help us out. My oldest sister, Alba Rocio, became a doctor. My youngest brother Ricardo, an engineer. My older brother Julian got married. My mother was able to send my youngest sister, Lina Maria, to university where she would later graduate as an engineer. I had been accepted into the dentistry program at a university far from my hometown, but we had no money to maintain my studies. I had to quit two months after the program started and return home to take on any menial job I could to help my mom.

My aunt, who arrived at Canada in the 1970s, offered to help me immigrate to Canada. I came to Canada in 1991 with no post-secondary education, zero English skill, and no money. I came to Canada under the Assisted Relatives category, so getting the visa was easy.

Canada needed factory workers so while still in Colombia I took a one-year apprenticeship program to learn a trade as a factory worker. This turned out to be worthless as when I came to Canada, the country was in the middle of a recession that had started in 1989 and would not end until 1992. Further, I had zero knowledge of any of Canada's official languages. The only job I could get was cleaning floors in restaurants. I did this for almost four years.

In my third year in Canada, I realized that I had to do something with my life given that I came from an educated family. But I had no idea what to do or study. My aunt suggested that I learn how to fix TVs because "she had a friend who was doing ok with that". I enrolled and six months later was asked to meet the Dean who told me that I was the worst student ever, and that I could never graduate with my incredibly low marks.

Back home, if anybody needed their TV fixed, we all would say that we can fix it –and somehow, we would. So, there I was: cleaning floors and not even able to fix a TV. I quit the studies with my morale on the floor. I decided to spend time really thinking about what I wanted to do. I knew the answer: international business with governments. However, I still did not speak English well enough, had no money, and was afraid to apply to university.

In the summer of 1996, I applied to Seneca College to study international trade. I was not accepted. As the restaurant where I was working as a cleaner was only a 15-minute walking distance from the college, every day, for ten consecutive days, I would go to the reception

"I tell friends and family that Canada is a country full of opportunities."

desk of the college and beg the receptionist to help me. This lovely lady would always reply, "Mauricio, I am just the receptionist and there is nothing I can do. There is me and below me, the cleaners. Learn more English and apply next year". For ten days I repeated this routine. On eleventh day, that lady asked me to do a test for her. It thought it was just an excuse to get rid of me, but I had nothing to lose. After a few questions, oral and written, she put a stamp on a document and said, "Congratulations Mauricio, you start the classes in two weeks". Since then, I have never given up. I graduated with high honours with two different diplomas: one in International Business Administration and another in Customs Administration. For most students, getting two diplomas could take five years. It took me three and I was top of the class. My friends still remind me that I never had time for them during those years. I was only focused on studying.

Once I was accepted at Seneca, I knew that I should have new aspirations. I came up with and wrote down a list of 32 goals (I could not afford a computer). Almost every day I would read them, talk about them, and visualize them in the way my mother taught me. Defining your goals allows you to think of a path; talking about your goals puts pressure on you to deliver; and visualization helps your mind find solutions in a strategic manner.

Everything that happens in the world can be either an opportunity or a threat. After a lot of newspaper and book reading, I realized that some of those goals could be combined. My list went from 32 to 20, then later to 10, and finally to just three objectives. My first goal was to better myself at all levels: emotionally, intellectually, physically, and financially. The second was to work in international trade with a government. And the last was to help immigrants as a way of paying back the country that adopted me. Although I have achieved all of these, I have not stopped with the latter.

Upon graduation from Seneca in 1997, one of my professors (Maurice Platero) helped me secure a three-month internship with the Government of Ontario's export development unit. I went on to work for a couple of years at a newly created unit at Seneca College that provided training to Canadian companies interested in doing business in Latin America. With only two years of experience, I was already meeting influential people and organizations involved in international trade. It was time for a university degree.

In 1999, I enrolled in the Business Management Program at Ryerson University. With credits from Seneca, I only needed two years of classes for Ryerson to grant me a degree. During this university period I was still working at a restaurant, this time as a part-time bartender and chef assistant, not cleaning floors anymore. The wages allowed me to send money to my mom and to cover half of my expenses. In 2001, I graduated from Ryerson top of the class. Now I was ready to go after more senior jobs in international trade.

Still bothered by the fact that I had failed the TV repair course, I decided to get a certificate in telecommunications from the University of Toronto. I graduated but did not want to work in that industry. The technical side is not for me, but I proved that I could do it—especially with proper English skills. Since 1999, after graduating from Ryerson, I have been fortunate to work in international trade, in the private, public, and educational sectors. The funny thing is that today, I am responsible for helping tech companies from Ontario export into the U.S., which is the biggest market in the world. In a way, technology includes television and all the software that goes into it. Not bad for someone who was the worst student in the TV repair course!

During my first five years in Canada, I lacked role models that would inspire me to find and seek my dreams. The receptionist at Seneca College changed my life. She saw potential in me and somehow was able to convince whoever was in charge to let me start the program.

I must mention also a former military man in my hometown, renowned for his wisdom. He taught me to always look for solutions. As a teenager, I was incredibly shy and overly awkward. One day, I had a problem, I don't remember what it was but despite my fears I managed to knock on his door. He asked what I needed, and I told him my problem. He said, "Come back next week". A week later I returned, and he said to me "Please tell me again why you are here?", and, again, I told him my problem. He said, "Come back next week". This exercise lasted four weeks, so the fifth time I told him that he must not care because he always forgot my problem. Then he said something that I will never forget. He said, "Mauricio, you always come here with problems. You never come with solutions. Come up with a solution and I will help you". That moment changed my approach to life.

I tell friends and family that Canada is a country full of opportunities. But we must first find our mission, use the resources available, and focus on achieving our goals.

Since coming to Canada, I always look for the solution. I stay positive and avoid negative thoughts and people. I help others whenever I can—because I can, and because others have helped me.

I would share the following with those who are new to Canada:

- Follow your dreams. If you don't have one, then think hard on what you wanted to do when you were a teenager and go for it.
- Write all your goals, visualize them, talk about them constantly.
- Read newspapers for opportunities and ideas to achieve those goals.
- Surround yourself with positive people.
- Set the bar higher (learn from those much higher in life than you).
- Help others whenever you can.

I partially agree with Bono that the world needs more Canada. Canadians have developed a more inclusionary and gentler approach to decision-making due to its history and desire to maintain a relationship with the monarchy. Our country was founded by people from different colonies who mostly came from France and England; countries that had a long history of animosity, wars, and monarchy. Canada's soft approach is appreciated worldwide but we are also criticized for our timidity.

A contrary example is the U.S., which was founded mostly by people focused on individual decision-making and boldness.

Advice to prospective new Canadians

For those who are thinking of immigrating to Canada I would tell them to stop reading the media from their home countries. Read the Canadian mainstream media so that you learn and understand the language, culture, and traditions of Canada

MAURICIO OSPINA

is an international marketing consultant and Hispanic community leader and philanthropist.

One Became Two

Almaz Desta

Ethiopia

Before I came to Canada, I had a beautiful life, great family, work, and friends. The weather in Ethiopia was lovely. I was happy. I worked as an executive secretary for the tax administration. It was a good job and a great environment, and I enjoyed my work. However, things in the country began to change. Because of the revolution there was violence and killing. That was the reason I ended up in Canada.

I chose Canada because my husband at the time moved to Canada first. When I arrived here, everything was different; The weather, the lifestyle, work, everything. When I lived in Ethiopia, I learned about Canada through my history class. I don't know why, but I always had a love for the country. Even when my friends used to talk about moving to America, I was always more interested in Canada. Of course, I didn't realize how cold it was going to be!

I finished the process and paperwork for immigrating to Canada while I was still back home. I remember that it was stressful. My husband initiated the process. He had fled as a refugee to Djibouti first and then eventually came to Canada. He then sponsored me to come through the family reunification process. I was interviewed, and, when everything was complete, I came to Italy and received my visa from there to come to Canada a couple of weeks later.

I arrived in Canada on December 8th. I will never forget that date because that is when everything changed. I saw snow when I got to the airport, and I was not ready for snow. I only had on a light jacket and some sandals, and it was so cold! I was so excited.

"When I talk about life in Canada, I tell my family and friends the truth. I tell them about the realities of life, including the struggles."

The first twelve months were very challenging. Everything was so different. The food was different, but I could handle that. However, I had a very hard time with the work environment and with communication. I really wanted to work as a secretary like I did back home, but that was impossible because of the communication barrier. So, when I did finally get a job, it required me to stand the whole day and I was not used to that. I remember crying all the time.

I became pregnant and things became even more difficult. I had morning sickness and I couldn't keep any food down. Transportation was challenging because of the snow. Everything seemed so hard. But by the end of the first twelve 12 months, I gave birth to my baby and then I was so happy. I can say that I was happy for the first time in Canada once I gave birth to my daughter.

Overall, I faced issues in my first five years

here, however the highlights were mostly connected to my daughter. I loved watching her grow up, and I was able to gain a lot of independence and confidence in my new country because of the things I needed to do to help raise her. I made new friends and was connected to the growing Ethiopian community in Toronto.

When you raise a child back home you have the support of a wide network of family and friends. While I did have some great friends here in Canada, it was nothing compared to what I would have had in Ethiopia. This was very challenging and isolating. As a new immigrant in Canada, you have to be everything. You are a mother, a wife, a worker, a cleaner... everything. This was very different from the lifestyle I had in Ethiopia.

After completing six months of maternity leave, my employer asked me to return to work. I explained that I was still breastfeeding and was not ready, but they were insistent. I refused to come back, so they fired me, and that created financial hardship. Eventually I had to find another job, so I put my daughter in daycare. She was constantly getting sick, so I had to stop working again. Things were often up and down during those years.

My daughter had the biggest impact on my life in Canada. After moving to Canada, my marriage ended so I was raising my daughter on my own. She was the only thing I was thinking of. I didn't care about myself, All I cared about was her well-being and making sure she did well in school and was happy. I had other family members come to Canada. My sister lived with me for many years, which was great. But overall, my life was my daughter. And now, all these years later, my life revolves around my grandchildren!

When I talk about life in Canada, I tell my family and friends the truth. I tell them about the realities of life, including the struggles. A lot of times people don't understand or believe me when I tell them about living here. That is because many friends back home think that life in Canada is very easy, and people want to come because of things like social services. However, when people move or visit here, then they finally understand. They see how hard I work and how busy I am, going from work to get my daughter from school as well as taking care of things at home. It can be a difficult life.

I have changed a lot since moving to Canada. When I was in Ethiopia, I was very young and carefree. Life in Canada has forced me to become more responsible. I see now how Canadian I have become. This is especially obvious when I go to visit Ethiopia. When I am in Ethiopia, I find myself very impatient with things like the pace of work and customer service, and gender norms. I have become so used to the fast-paced life here and expect efficient service when I am visiting an office or business. So, in some ways I have become less patient.

Overall, my journey has been positive. The weather has always been hard to get used to and there were many challenges along the way. However, immigrating is an opportunity to learn and grow in many ways. Focusing on communication as well as finding and contributing to a community has been so important. For me, my church was such a valuable community for me during this journey.

Advice to prospective new Canadians

I would tell someone who is thinking of coming to Canada not to be too excited or have any particular expectations, good or bad. Just come and face it. Come and face the reality, whatever that is going to be for you. Before you come here, do whatever you can to prepare or adjust once you get here.

The last thing I would add is that if you come to Canada, do try and go to school as soon as you are able. Otherwise, go to work, find an activity, play sports, or attend church. Just don't stay home. Make friends and stay active.

ALMAZ DESTA

is a hardworking and happy grandmother who continues to live in Canada. Her faith and family remain the bedrock that keeps her grounded.

It Wasn't an Easy Landing

Eni Oszlai

Germany

June 11, 2004, was the day I boarded a plane in Düsseldorf, Germany headed for Toronto a city in Canada. Two of my closest friends came with me to the airport to hug me; 'See you later'. It was a big decision. Not only did I plan to immigrate to a different country and continent, leaving my life as I knew it behind, but I was heading to my Canadian fiancé to marry him and start a new life. Life that day was full of hope, light, and love.

A week later, my parents arrived from Europe to spend some time with us before the wedding. It felt like a great family vacation. Our wedding day was filled with sunshine, beauty, love, and laughter. We danced well past midnight, and everybody had a great time.

Shortly after, we started my immigration process from within Canada. What did it mean? I could not leave the country—not even for the funeral of my grandparents who passed away just months apart shortly after my arrival in Canada. What I could do is to use my time wisely: to study and volunteer. During this time, I completed my Business Communication Certificate and gained valuable work experience as a volunteer that helped me to land my first opportunity a year later at the Canadian Securities Institute.

It wasn't an easy landing. By profession, I was a teacher with a university degree, and had been working in the world of finance and project management in various leadership roles, including the rollout of a multibillion-dollar international merger of a business law firm headquartered in the U.K. and Germany. In Canada, my foreign credentials were fully acknowledged on paper; however, to be employable, I needed to obtain that most wanted" Canadian Experience".

"I am grateful that Canada has given me the opportunity to make a difference!"

After I completed my first year of my first paid job in the financial sector and had taken additional courses, I was ready to move on. My next opportunity was with one of the largest Canadian insurance companies. Initially, I worked with them in a customer service role, and shortly after, I advanced to manage multimillion-dollar pension plans. I was making a difference in the lives of thousands of people by helping them build their future from a financial perspective. In addition, I completed my Master's in Adult Education. I felt that I wanted to do more and multiply the good I was creating.

During this time, I became a mom. I waited 33 years for this miracle. First, we welcomed our precious little daughter and four years later our beautiful son. This was the pinnacle of the journey to the New World, only to be rattled by a major car accident. The financial consequences of not having an adequate 'Plan B' were dire. Credit card balances crept up, and we needed to refinance our mortgage. This was a major wakeup call. Investments alone don't do the trick. More holistic solutions are needed for all. I knew I had to tell my story and educate others. While my body was healing, my mind became restless. This experience inspired me to become the financial doctor that I am today. I obtained all my financial licenses for investments, insurance, and real estate. I also completed a business and mindset coaching certification program.

Once I was ready to re-enter the workforce, I wanted to make sure that I would work for a company that was financially strong, was Canadian, and represented my values and integrity. Soon I became a leader and role model within my organization.

I am most grateful for my clients and business partners for allowing me to do what I love and enjoy: to empower others to make their dreams and vision a tangible reality!

Because of my love of music, I got involved with Global Citizen, an organization involved on a global scale addressing humanitarian and environmental issues.

My journey has afforded me the opportunity to become successful and to give back. Today, I support several charities. I also provide guidance and empowerment to musicians, so that their art can reach the masses. My book, The Toronto Waterfront Awards: Powerful Success Stories, became a bestseller in 2020, as it served as an inspiration for others to use their mindset to create the life they desired. My podcast, The Financial Doctor Show, has attracted trailblazers who are able to tell their story and give light and hope to others.

My new partnership as a publisher for Empowering Women to Succeed highlights the journey of others and nurtures the next generation of legacy builders.

I am grateful that Canada has given me the opportunity to make a difference!

Advice to prospective new Canadians

Canada's multiculturalism is a major asset and opportunity for new immigrants. This is a welcoming country, allowing its residents to thrive and find countless opportunities to give back to others—over time. Be ready to learn and to contribute. Bring a positive mindset, a relentless attitude to succeed, and the desire to make a difference. Create your roadmap for success. You will discover that the entire world can live happily together in the same neighbourhood, as Canada creates a safe and supportive environment for everyone to thrive. I encourage you to practice Love and Gratitude to manifest your Dreams all along the way!

ENI OSZLAI

is an award-winning financial doctor, RBC's top financial specialist in Canada, mother of two, a bestselling author, speaker, podcast host, publisher, and philanthropist.

I Held on to Hope and Optimism

Kamini Sahadeo

Guyana

As years go by and we get the chance to open our eyes wide, we realized that "people will forget what you said, people will forget what you did, but people will never forget how you made them feel," (Maya Angelou). This was an aha moment for me as it summarizes in one line that the way we are treated greatly shapes and affects our lives.

A precis of my career as a Guyanese immigrant in Canada will set some context for my story. I started my career in financial services, followed by a transition to public service by volunteering in policy development on political campaigns. Thereafter, I worked as a public service worker for a federal Member of Parliament. I now work as a workforce development consultant and teach at the post-secondary level in the areas of human resources and non-profit management.

Immediately upon completing my undergraduate and graduate studies in International Relations at the university in Birmingham, U.K., I applied for permanent residency in Canada. As with any major life event, a move to an entirely new country brought new challenges. However, in hindsight, such events led to personal growth and development. Support of my aunts, uncles, and cousins living in Toronto mitigated the transition challenges. One aunt allowed me to stay with her for several months until I could afford to live on my own.

"Canadians have a reputation around the world for being open, welcoming, approachable."

There were many job opportunities in Toronto, Ontario for new graduates without work experience. I initially sought work in my area of interest and qualifications but soon realized that I needed to broaden my search. I began exploring options and eventually got a full-time customer service role with a major Canadian bank, where I was fortunate to stay for another fifteen years in roles of progressive responsibility. I must confess, I had not expected it to take so long to move up the ranks to a role that was commensurate with my aptitude, interests, and qualifications.

Culturally and socially, Canadians have a reputation around the world for being open, welcoming, approachable. I have found this attitude to be very contagious and is one that I have easily adopted upon arriving here. But first, I experienced a little culture shock. Having lived and worked in several countries before, I still was not prepared for such a work-dominated life in Canada as working long hours leaves little time for family, friends, and social activities. Thus, I felt some social isolation at the beginning, but then I, too, started to dedicate extra time to professional development and building networks outside of my job.

It is crucial to always remember that you alone can't win life's race. At each stage, there are always people who become a catalyst for your success. For me, the biggest impact has been the support of mentors, relatives, and close friends. From a career perspective, I have been fortunate to have worked for and with the most generous and supportive individuals who have opened doors, dedicated time, shared their wisdom and insights, and become friends for life.

With the kindest intentions, I should also mention that there are always areas that can be improved. Yes, Canada is a country I have always admired for its position on human rights, peacekeeping, neutrality, and being the honest broker. I think the world needs the generosity of spirit that Canadians have. However, while Canadian society and workplaces are advancing at being inclusive of newcomers and the various cultures, I think more can be done to reflect the best of what each one brings to the table at all levels. Moreover, to thrive in the future economy, Canada must be a lot more innovative, creative, and comfortable with taking risks.

Overall, throughout my life journey, Canada has become for me what the American dream is for millions of people. Every down is followed by an up, and results are worth the initial challenges. After moving to Canada, I reconnected and bonded with long-lost family members and friends, became a citizen, learned more about the country and the people, became financially and personally independent. Most importantly, I learned that I should also mentor and help others as I have been helped. No matter where we will end up, all we remember are those people who warmed our hearts and mitigated our suffering. I strongly believe that people define every country and culture. These emotions were exactly that aha moment that made me appreciate and enjoy all of the four seasons of our life.

"I think the world needs the generosity of spirit that Canadians have."

Advice to prospective new Canadians

The greatest insight I would like to share is that it's important to hold on to that sense of hope and optimism accompanying you when you first arrive here. There will be ups and downs, maybe more downs than ups at first, and it is important to seek support. Being surrounded by peers from a similar culture may temporarily mitigate the fears and anxiety, but only until it starts to separate you from the rest of the society. To avoid exclusion, you should acquire knowledge and skills, widen the network of professionals to access opportunities, and become a part of the society. Yes, the weather is sometimes harsh, but let us fully embrace it and, with the right clothing and planning, we can thrive in it!

KAMINI SAHADEO

is a professor and consultant in workforce development and non-profit management. She is also an active volunteer and serves on the boards of several non-profit organizations.

A Citizen of the World Chooses to be a Citizen of Canada

Gautam Nath

Egypt

My name is Gautam Gordon Nath. I am a very multicultural person as my dad was from India and worked for the Indian High Commission as a diplomat. My mum was from Prague, Czech Republic; my sister was born in London, U.K.; my brother in New Delhi India; and myself in Cairo, Egypt. As young kids, we traveled through different countries with dad, including a stint in the city of Ottawa in Canada during my formative early teen years. This love for Canada brought me back many years later as a permanent resident and now a Canadian citizen.

My dad retired and we moved to New Delhi, India. I started university, going on to complete my Master's in Business Administration. Over the years, I was able to move up the corporate ladder to the board of directors for a global multinational agency, the WPP Group. I have traveled to over 35 countries and 150 cities across the globe. If it had been feasible, I would have tried extra-terrestrial travel, but guess some things are yet to come.

My area of expertise was marketing and, before leaving for Canada, I was honoured to be recognized as one of India's Top 100 Marketing Professionals. Life was good, and I had no real complaints. However, as a global traveler, I did want to have the experience of being a citizen in one of the world's best places. This desire started us on a journey towards Canada. One that took all of five and a half years to complete and I am proud to be a Canadian citizen today.

"If you let things get you down, you end up in a downward spiral."

The wait for PR status was five and a half years and that was very long. Our life was on hold during that time. We did not want to invest in anything as we did not know when the call would come. Because of that, we did not start a family, but then found life too complicated even after we landed to start a family hence that was a milestone missed.

Today the queue is far shorter. People can now get their permanent residency before they have really understood the full implications of such a move. Other than the long and uncertain wait, everything else went smoothly.

We came to visit twice as tourists while we waited for our PR to materialize. We were able to experience the lovely lakes, the fresh air, the green forests, abundant food and drink, birds, butterflies, and such warm, friendly, and happy people. We arrived as landed immigrants and Canada was our new home. Suddenly we saw something different, We now saw the cracks on the sidewalks, the homeless on the streets, graffiti on walls, despair in people's eyes, and the poor state of the job market. Canada had not changed, but our perspective did.

In the early months, we decided not to be in a hurry to find jobs but to spend quality time understanding the lay of the land, much like a general who sends out his scouts to do a reconnaissance before committing troops. I spent hours on the TTC till I had a good idea of the city and how it was spread out. Those hours on the subway helped me understand who lived in the city, how they dressed, and how they carried themselves. I joined several networking groups for professionals and volunteered at organizations. I also began to contribute articles, start mentorship groups, and learn how life in Toronto could be. I joined Goodlife Fitness to start a routine and stay fit during the cold winter. Further I attended various cultural events once the weather warmed up and took time to experience some cottage country getaways. This was all to assimilate and become a good member of society.

One of my first highlights here occurred within eight months. After a gruelling two-hour interview, I was selected by CBC Television to be featured on The National, a very famous program hosted by the Canadian icon, Peter Mansbridge. The segment was called Becoming Canadian and was broadcast on Canada Day. I was barely eight months in the country and was beamed across the nation on the most important day of the year, Canada Day!

I remember the CBC camera crew was in my office to shoot some clips and Michael Adams, the leader of the company at that time, came to me and said, "Gautam, in my 30 years of running this organization, a CBC camera crew has never been in my office, but in three months of you being here, you have them visiting".

The next milestone was getting my articles on multicultural marketing published in the media. I started some mentorship groups, a blog, and a regular magazine column titled Building Your Brand that ran for 24 issues.

In 2011, I was recognized as one of Canada's Top 25 Immigrants. A proud moment indeed. I also started my company, Multicultural Marketing Solutions Canada, to help organizations to gain strategic insights into the fast-growing multicultural communities especially South Asian and Asian cohorts.

However, it was not all easy. Having had corporate success and recognition back in my home country, I arrived here a mere statistic, immigrant number 123. No one knows you and no one cares about your past. It's all about what you have done here and how it is relevant to Canadians. The older you are, the faster you must move once you arrive. The higher you are on the corporate ladder before you come, the more rungs lower you must start.

Everyone is so busy running against their own challenges that they don't have time for you. If you let things get you down, you end up in a downward spiral and that leads to depression and negative vibrations. If you stay positive and have patience, then things slowly improve.

The other challenge is the pace of things; many of us come from much faster-paced countries where you must constantly be on the move and aggressively work to stay on top. If you stop, you will be surpassed by others and get left behind. The pace in Canada is far slower and more laidback. New professionals like us are changing the equilibrium and helping Canada to hold our own in the global arena.

We are no longer under the shadow of our Big Brother to the south. We must grow up and stand on our own feet. There are initial teething issues that professional new Canadian's face. What struck me over the years since coming here is the glass ceiling (negative) and the improved calibre (positive) of the new immigrant population.

No longer are farmers and oil field workers coming. They are being replaced by the educated professional. We are the jewel in Canada's crown and harnessing our energy, global knowledge and wisdom is what will make all the difference.

My challenge is to help make this happen. I continue to spend time, energy, and resources to enact this change. Bringing educated international professionals in senior levels to government and private organizations is paramount for Canada's future.

There is gentle, subtle resistance and my role is to showcase that we are here and more then able to bring about positive change. Open the doors to us and utilize our skills to fast-track Canada's economic and intellectual progress. This resistance has had the biggest impact on me since landing. In my journey there have been many well-wishers and believers but also a few naysayers.

"The pace in Canada is far slower and more laidback."

When family and friends ask me about Canada, I tell them that it is not all milk and honey. Money is not everything and you need to be grateful for an improved quality of life in terms of peace, quiet, education, healthcare, and an abundance of fresh air and nature. Coming from a highly populated country, we were used to having domestic help as it was affordable. This is not available here. We had to learn to do many chores like cooking, cleaning, and laundry. But in the reverse, we get nature and fresh clean air to breathe. Our children grow up in this clean and safe environment and have the potential to become leading citizens of the country.

Yes, we don't meet friends as often but with social media proliferation, the world is our teacup. Today, living in the shadow of Covid-19, we are learning a new way of living and how to live a more virtual life.

There is struggle in finding meaningful jobs, handling transition periods between jobs, and in staying ahead of the game. If your yardstick of success is overall quality of life rather than money, your level of gratitude will reflect it.

Since coming to Canada, I have been taught many lessons including:

- Giving back is a way of life, not a choice if you want to progress.
- Learning to live in peace with multicultural communities both in my social and professional life.
- Money is not everything
- To be happy and grateful for what God has given us.
- Learning politeness, patience, and the art of reflection.

I came to Canada, a landed immigrant like any other. No contacts or network but with a decent bank balance. I continue to address the challenges but move forward with a positive commitment to making a difference.

Advice to prospective new Canadians

If I could offer advice to new immigrants, I would tell them not to forget friends and family back home. Don't sever those ties. Continue to respect your elders as the western culture supports independence which leads to isolation of the elders. This should change. Embrace change and be open to it. This is a new environment so step away from your safety zone and take risks and respect others' space. Lower your expectations and be prepared to give before you get. Be wary in your spending. Settle in slowly and steadily and remember, there are many who will be after your dollar. Smile and have a positive attitude, but do not wait for things to come to you. Go out and be proactive.

GAUTAM NATH

is a senior marketing and corporate strategy professional. He was recognized as Canada's Top 25 Immigrants, Canada's Top 50 Board Diversity Professionals, a Citizenship Oath Presiding Officer and the recipient of the Sovereigns Medal. He lives with his wife Vineeta in Toronto.

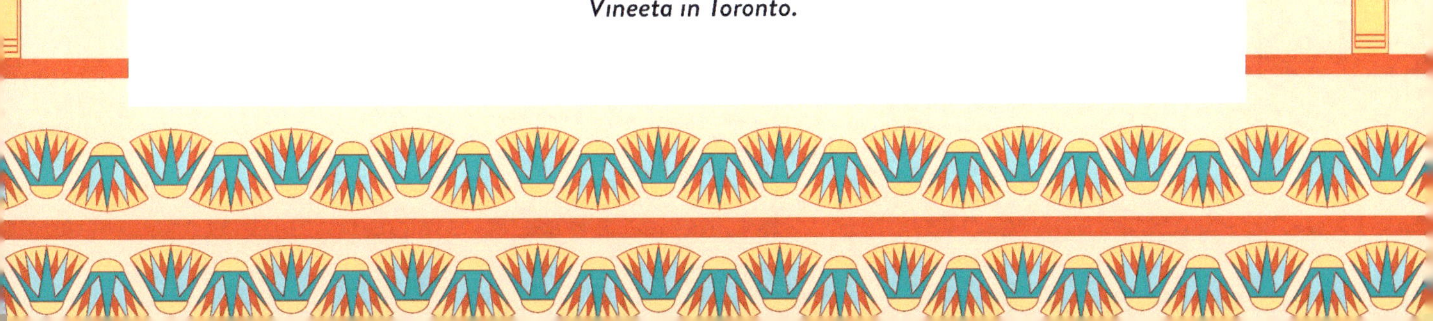

One Foot in Canada

Jos Nolle

Holland

I was born in Holland, the Netherlands, in December 1955. I was the youngest of three kids. At the time, Holland was a real welfare state. It did not occur to me how sheltered I was until 1980 during an Internship in South Africa. At the time, South Africa was still under the apartheid's regime, which for me was an eye-opener, and solidified the idea that the world was a much more complicated place than I had first assumed.

I completed my master's degree, specifically for Industrial Design Engineers and decided to travel around the world for a year. I took out a $25,000 loan to finance the trip, with my parents as a guarantor. When I returned to Holland, I was fortunate to land a job in marketing and sales with an aircraft manufacturer. In 1984, there were about 600 staff in the division and a total of about 15,000 other employees. After five years, I made a significant career change. It was my initial goal to get a job with the United Nations Development Program (UND), however, by sheer coincidence, I ended up working with Doctors Without Borders (also known as MSF - Médecins Sans Frontieres) in what was then one of its largest medical relief programs in war-torn Mozambique.

In the late 1989 (halfway through my two-year contract with MSF) I decided to get married. That was the start of my life and my work in Canada. My wife is Dutch-Canadian

"Since coming to Canada, I have become even more open-minded about international complexities than ever before."

and early in our marriage we lived for two years in Holland with our two young kids. My wife missed her family, so we returned to Canada in 1995, where I started to look for new work.

After getting married, I started the application process for PR status, which took about a year. I found it an easy process, but the immigration officer did ask me some weird and surprising questions about my travels. For example, he asked if I had carried or smuggled drugs during my travels in Southeast Asia. I have never been interested in becoming a Canadian citizen. I am genuinely Dutch. As a permanent resident, I have the same rights and duties as other Canadians, and I am a happy taxpayer. My wife still rolls her eyes when I say it. I cannot vote, but that is fine as I know there are no true social-democratic parties in Canada.

Before I came to Canada in late 1990, the MSF Holland section had asked me to set up a Canadian division and to start recruiting doctors, nurses, and logisticians. I started that project as a volunteer in Canada until I got my PR status in 1991. By that time, we had successfully incorporated MSF Canada as a new non-governmental organization (NGO). I was the first employee on their payroll. This was an excellent opportunity for me to get to know more about Canada. Thanks to the expense budget from MSF Holland, I visited several cities in Ontario as well as Victoria, Vancouver BC; Edmonton, AB; Montreal, Quebec; and Halifax, Nova Scotia. I probably have seen more of Canada in my first few years here than most Canadians. It was a very good experience despite the early situations of mild culture shock during that time.

I was in Canada from September 1990 to December 1992. I returned to Amsterdam to join the management team of MSF Holland, where I worked between 1993 and 1994. I came back to Canada in January 1995 and started my job search. I felt I had a solid education and 13-14 years of valuable professional experience. I sent out roughly 100 letters to companies, most were responses to job postings or unsolicited letters. Not one resulted in an interview. I reached out to some HR professionals in Toronto who proceeded to tell me that I was a "hard to sell" individual. My work experience was challenging to explain. People had a difficult time understanding what work I had done during my years with FOKKER (Dutch airline manufacturer) and MSF. Some people said that the work with MSF was not seen as serious professional work. It was disheartening to hear, and it made me sad. I felt that I was ready to go back to Holland, but my wife convinced me to stay. Her sister was an ESL (English as a Second Language) teacher at Niagara College, and the college was looking for a new director to expand its international portfolio.

I was hesitant to apply for that position at Niagara College because of my own post-secondary learning experiences. I was a poor performing student due to my ineptitude in memorizing things such as numbers and formulas. I didn't have much to lose. I applied and was offered a position and after earning well over $100,000 per year with FOKKER, then just $10,000 per year with MSF for years, and about $70,000 as the director HR and Training with MSF Holland, I accepted a starting salary of $42,000 with Niagara College. I was never motivated by, nor cared much about, wages, but the experience of the job search in my late thirties did somewhat taint my early impressions of Canada. The country does seem very welcoming but there are darker realities for newcomers once they start looking for meaningful employment. I was shocked by how close-minded the decision-makers of companies were at the time. I think the job environment is a bit better now. Just as shocking is how right of center all politics in Canada seem to be. Although much better than the U.S., it is surprising for somebody from northern Europe who grew up in communities with stronger social democracy roots.

Some additional challenges I found during my first few years in Canada were finding a happy balance with the family of my Dutch Canadian wife. My in-laws both came to Canada in their early twenties soon after the end of the Second World War which had left the European continent in ruins. My wife and her two siblings were born and raised in Canada and the whole family was of course fully adjusted to the Canadian way of life. Initially I stubbornly wanted to instill some more current Dutch values in our two kids even though I realized from the beginning that they would most likely live their lives in Canada. I compromised by allowing our kids to be on their bicycles in our neighborhood without wearing helmets (but they were not allowed to tell their mother). That may sound like a silly example, but such things were important for me during my time of adaptation. Canadian society had developed, with good reason, some different values than what I had growing up in Holland. Neither are better than the other, just different, and as a new parent it meant greater effort to find a balance.

I find that the so called neo-liberal movement had much more impact in North America than in most of the European countries. There also appears to be remnants of the pioneer survival-of-the-fittest mentality. Although there is less and less with each new generation. I tell all my friends that, as with many other new immigrants,

"I have one foot in Canada and one foot in Europe."

I have one foot in Canada and one foot in Europe. Still, my children are wholly Canadian, and that's fine. I have no regrets coming here, but I do love going back to Holland regularly. I am lucky that my work travel routes send me through Amsterdam quite frequently. I must also say that eating habits are quite inadequate in Canada compared to Europe, where fresh food has always been the main staple. I also find the good folks in Canada to be a bit more superficial while the Dutch love to dive right into your personal life. I think somewhere in the middle would be the right balance.

Since coming to Canada, I have become even more open-minded about international complexities than ever before. However, I must admit I am still a Dutch guy having a good time in Canada. I try to be as respectful as possible. Nevertheless, I often upset my Canadian colleagues or friends unintentionally. I blame it on my darn Dutch bluntness.

Advice to prospective new Canadians

The main lesson of what I'm saying is that it is essential to have patience with yourself and your new fellow citizens. As newcomers we must learn to adjust as others need time to learn about us and where we come from. Refugees come full of trauma. Although I really didn't experience trauma, I would get upset if people in Canada did not show empathy for situations I had witnessed during my time in Mozambique. I have learned to hide my feelings and become more realistic about the reactions of those with whom I still sometimes share experiences.

JOS NOLLE

sees himself as a new immigrant (after more than 25 years in Canada) who did not leave his native homeland because of economic or safety reasons, but instead to be with the woman who has become his life partner.

Two Journeys...One Destination

Bala and Karnika Krishnan

India

"I had to deal with racism."

Bala and Karnika—a married couple—had different journeys but met similar obstacles.

Bala: I graduated in chemical engineering from the University of Madras, India. I worked as an engineer at a lubricant plant in India for a brief period. Since my school days, I have been fascinated with Canada, its people, environment, and the opportunity it offers for gas and oil engineers.

Bala: I graduated in chemical engineering from the University of Madras, India. I worked as an engineer at a lubricant plant in India for a brief period. Since my school days, I have been fascinated with Canada, its people, environment, and the opportunity it offers for gas and oil engineers.

Karnika: I graduated in home science at Sayajirao University at Baroda, India. I worked as an early childhood educator in Kenya, East Africa (my original home) and I was quite successful there. During this period the school expanded, and they wanted my services at a higher level such as a supervisor but my application for immigration to Canada was accepted. I felt the strong need to leave, and I did not consider working in Kenya as paramount.

Bala: Canada fascinated me as a country with its vast expanse and its richness of natural resources. I had visions of working or starting a business in my chosen professional field. The pristine appearance of Canada and the abundance of opportunity was very attractive. My age (26 at the time) was also helpful in my choosing Canada because of my explorative nature.

Karnika: I studied geography and I was fascinated with Canada's nature, vast openness, and the Indigenous peoples. I was impressed with what Canada had to offer in the field of early childhood education. My approach to education was one of helping people who were disadvantaged both financially and physically. I applied my skills in childhood development both in Africa and India. I wanted to bring these skills to Canada as well because the opportunity to help was immense. I recognized that a need was also there. My fascination with Canada as an unspoiled, clean country attracted me here.

Bala: After landing in Canada as an immigrant I realized that there was a disconnect between my vision and reality. I was disappointed on several fronts.

- The Canadian Embassy in New Delhi did not tell me that my credentials were not equivalent or what I needed to prepare for what lay ahead. They were quick to issue the immigrant visa without preparing me at length about the new life here.

- I had to deal with racism. It was a new experience in a bad way, which I did not expect. I feel that racism in Canada is like an ugly pimple on the beautiful face of this country.
- My credentials were treated as equivalent to a high school diploma. This was a total insult and I felt it was utter disrespect for the hard work I did to earn my degree. The university in India used the same education system as here and the textbooks were the same and the rigorous requirements were the same as in any Canadian university. The professional body in Canada insisted that I do my engineering in Canada if I wanted to practice my profession.

Karnika: My education was accepted as equivalent when I applied to work as an early childhood educator. I considered myself lucky. At first, I worked pro-bono to get "Canadian Experience". Later I learned that this requirement was an excuse not to hire people of a different colour. Nevertheless, I went through the tough times and came through and proved my worth to the potential employer. I studied at Seneca college to upgrade my skills and further my qualifications. Things went smoothly from there. The Toronto municipal government was prepared to accept me for employment. I disliked the racist aspect of the employment, but it did not hinder my performance much because the environment was more open to immigrants.

Bala: The first 12 months were quite rough. I contemplated returning to India to start my life again. However, at that point I met Karnika, and things turned around for the better. My job search continued to be hampered by racist attitudes and negative judgement of my experience and knowledge.

Karnika: The fact that I was working with no or little income and managing the new environment and new culture made the first year very difficult. But I steadfastly hung in there because I believed that there was a future for me in Canada. In retrospect, I was right.

Bala: Even though I experienced various difficulties during my first year or two, I had to hold many menial jobs just to earn a living, but it was a worthwhile lesson in humility. I put myself through The University of Toronto and Karnika had a major part to play in it. She worked hard to support me financially. The highlight during the first five years was to work as a stock trade assistant at the Toronto Stock Exchange for Merrill Lynch Pierce

"The exposure to Canadian life was refreshing."

Fenner Smith. It introduced me to the vagaries of the investment world. I am thankful for such an opportunity. Looking back, I can say unequivocally that it helped pave the way for my future. I began to appreciate the importance of saving and investment. From this point forward, I never looked back.

Karnika: After meeting Bala within the first year or two of my arrival, my life became smooth sailing. The demands of employment, and the intricacies of dealing with the public and their children's education was quite demanding and different than my experience in either Kenya or India. The learning curve was quite steep. It became apparent that furthering my education and learning various aspects of my work was the only way to success. Seneca College played an important role in that regard.

Bala: In those first five years the challenge was to face the hurdles related to my education equivalency and getting accreditation from the Professional Engineers of Ontario. To top it all, I had to go to university and repeat the same subjects that I did once before. I realized that even after graduation there was no guarantee of employment because I faced racism every which way I turned. Racism is the cancer in this society. This aspect of Canada left a bad taste, even to this day. By accident I discovered computers and the software industry. It was a natural affinity for me; I was like a fish taking to water. Personal computers were coming into vogue, and it was perfect for me. My career switched from being a chemical engineer to a computer hardware/software specialist. At first blush I felt these two fields were poles apart. But I quickly recognized parallels in both fields such as the need for knowledge in mathematics and science. Most of what I know in the computer field is self-taught. I did not I find the need to attend any college to learn the field, nor did I have any mentors.

Karnika: I met Bala within the first two years of my arrival. We quickly discovered our compatibility and agreed to get married. I had the responsibility of earning and helping my husband go to university to finish what he set out to do. We decided at this point that the struggle was much more than we realized, so, we put our plans of raising a family in abeyance. The aspect of raising children did not take high priority in our lives. We enjoyed each other's company and we enjoyed traveling with our limited resources. It gave us immense pleasure. As the years rolled by, having a little Bala or a little Karnika was not in our cards. My career was blooming, and I enjoyed working with children and the challenge of dealing with the public. I asked for, and received, help from my superiors. At some point in my career, I wanted to be in an administrative capacity, but my biggest obstacle was to switch how I dealt with things culturally from Indian to Canadian. To be successful, certain aspects of aggressiveness and

"Appreciation of other religions and cultures without compromising your own beliefs."

assertiveness were required to deal with certain aspects of the job. My personality was not conducive to such an approach. Therefore, I did not pursue this avenue further. I also sensed racial overtones at higher levels of management which prevented me from engaging in various pursuits. The hierarchy of a government employment also came with certain quirks that I was not quite prepared to explore to any great extent.

Neither Bala or I were mentored when we came. As a result, we are attempting to correct this situation, or lack of it, by being mentors to chosen young people. We recognized very early on such youngsters needed help to plant their feet in Canada and we know and firmly believe that they do have plenty of chances to succeed in the future. We play the roles of advisors to those who wish to talk to us about life in Canada. We place heavy emphasis on youth, education, and staying employed.

Bala and Karnika: We do not go into great details about our first few years of Canada to family and friends as they were not very good. We do speak about better opportunities, cleaner living, and higher standards of living compared with where we came from. We relate some of our experiences with regards to technology, science, and general living. There is freedom of speech, congregation, religion, thought, and actions. We tell them this kind of freedom also bears responsibility and one should work within this frame. Nothing is handed out on a silver platter, and one has to be forever thankful for choosing Canada as their new home if the quality of life they leave behind is any less than the one they intend to adopt. We tell them to be aware that umping from the fryer into the fire is akin to leaving for Canada without a set, clear plan that will lead to a reasonable path to success.

Bala and Karnika: We both recognized the value in our culture. We did not change our ways to just to fit in as Canadians. However, there are a lot of positives about Canadian society: Mutual respect; Helpfulness; Appreciation of other religions and cultures without compromising your own beliefs. We had to dress differently but have adapted as it is conducive to the weather here and it is a lot more practical. We did not find that people, in general, are any different than those we left behind. We realized the richness of staying in touch with our roots and never giving up what we practiced and preached. Respect for others, believing in yourself and being proud of your culture are important values for us.

Bala and Karnika: Coming to Canada as an immigrant is not a ticket to wealth or an easy life by any means. If one is prepared to go through with the initial teething troubles, the rewards are there. Do not come here with an attitude that somehow, someone, somewhere, owes you something. Work for it. Earn it. Nothing comes easy without the sweat of one's brow. If you are prepared to work hard and diligently, then the rewards of a better life will happen. The place one leaves behind may lack opportunity. If that is so, choose Canada because challenges related to hard work lie ahead. Rewards are a natural outcome.

Karnika: Have an aim. Just like one navigates a map, know where you want to be within what duration.

Bala and Karnika: Landing in a new place demands some unique requirements. In that regard, Canada is no exception. Going to a place blindly with no road map spells disaster for one's career. Set a goal. Know how realistic it is and the parameters of whether you can achieve it given your own cultural background and ethnicity. We learned how important it is to be nimble and flexible without giving up on what you set out to do.

As Canadians, we believe in quietly doing a lot of things that go relatively unnoticed. Our psyche as Canadians is to do without bragging. We leave that up to others. We are serious about offers of help, and we do it with zero expectations.

"Our psyche as Canadians is to do without bragging."

Yes, the world needs more Canada. We are quietly efficient. The sad fact is, if we win the Stanley Cup, World Series or NBA Championship, our neighbours to the south do not make even a whimper of recognition. In stark contrast, we selflessly assisted our neighbours whenever they were in difficulty. Whether it was assisting passengers after 911, first responders during forest fires in California or flood waters in Florida, we do so without asking for anything in return. We swallow our pride.

Bala and Karnika: We have a great deal of advice to give potential immigrants. If they are in a certain high level in their employment or business that can provide a happy life, we advise them: "Stay-Where-You-Are". Do not think for a minute that it will be any better in Canada than what you intend to leave. If you have any visions of getting rich quick or only have a materialistic outlook to life, then Canada is not for you.

Who should come to Canada? If you are young, or have a young family, have excellent educational qualifications, or experience that this country can use, and you are confident that you can contribute, then apply for an immigrant visa. And after receiving it through proper channels, pack your bags and embark on a journey to Canada. We want you. You will be successful here because opportunity is plentiful, but you must be prepared to work hard. We recognize talented people and reward them adequately.

Do a lot of homework before you start. Is your skill set saleable in Canada? Is your spouse supportive of your efforts? Is she/he prepared to go through the trials and tribulations that this new life will inevitably bring? Do you have a road map, an aim? Within what time frame do you want to achieve it? How realistic is it? Can you work in a remote location in Canada? Are you afraid of unknown, new things? How honest are you with your answers? And, finally, do not depend on anybody such as your aunt, uncle, nephew, or other relatives living here. They have their own fires to put out. You should not be an additional burden to them however welcoming they may be. If you do accept their help, pay back in one form or other or pay it forward.

Canadians are polite. We respect your views, and we are a democratic nation. Some things you hear in Canadian politics may be shocking at first, especially if you have grown up in a non-democratic environment. You are intelligent enough to discern the differences very quickly. You will feel you belong here. If you keep the head low and let the bullets fly - you will like it here.

We, Bala and Karnika, are Canadian. We are part and parcel of this nation in every way. We are part of its fabric. And yet, we are proud of our heritage and culture, and we do not forget where we came from. In general, we live an enriched life. We believe we have the best of both worlds: The one we were born into and the one we adopted willingly.

Advice to prospective new Canadians

Learn not to take everything at face value; do your own due diligence. Trust but verify. Don't be afraid to ask questions. Know your rights. Respect the law. Do not ever be on the wrong side of the law - it will ruin your life here in Canada.

When confronted with heavy criticism, argument, or character assassination, agree to disagree. There are a lot of merits to such an approach. It may not be so apparent in your country, but in Canada, such an approach is prudent, and it works. Less is more agreement. No one wins by the attitude might is right and your way or the highway.

Religion in your life is important. Being fanatical about your belief will upset a lot of people in Canada because here we respect each other's beliefs, way of living, and way of dress. We observe a lot of etiquette here.

Canada is a peaceful country. We are so thankful to Canada for giving us a home. There is room for everyone in this country. Don't let anyone steer you wrong or make you feel unwelcome. Canada does have a race problem; we must discuss it openly for it to get better.

I Obtained What I Could Not Predict

Maksim Sokolov

Uzbekistan

My goal had always been to become a Canadian citizen. In 2007, I embarked on my journey.

Before coming to Canada, I received a Ph.D. in Mathematics and worked as an assistant professor at the National University of Uzbekistan. I was also an adjunct professor of mathematics at Moscow State University, and I worked as a part-time analyst at the Consulate of Canada, which is where I met several Canadian diplomats. They taught all about the country and encouraged me to apply for permanent residence. At that time, the wait time was long, but I was prepared.

After a research trip to Cardiff University in the U.K, I received an offer to move there as a postdoctoral researcher at Cardiff University. During that time, I received my invitation to move to Canada as a permanent resident—which came much faster than I could anticipate.

This presented a serious dilemma to me: should I move to Canada or work at Cardiff until the end of my research assignment and lose the offer to become Canadian? At that time, I based my decision on the many stories I had heard about the country and on my assumption that Canada would offer me and my family many more opportunities and much more stability than I could have if I did not move. The move was on! I realize now that I saw many things with rose-tinted glasses.

"I have changed since moving to Canada. I now appreciate the stability and calmness."

Ultimately, I did not make a mistake by moving to Canada. I began to love Canada in different ways than I had anticipated. Many things which I thought would happen in Canada, did not, but conversely, many things which I did not think about—did. So, I moved based on the ideas which were not fully correct; at the same time, I obtained what I could not have predicted.

The process was very simple. I filled in papers and sent them to the embassy. I expected the decision to take time, based on the wait times I had read about. However, the application went through very quickly. When I arrived, I chose Toronto, Ontario, as my home base. I didn't know anyone except several diplomates who I previously met at the Canadian Consulate and who lived in Ottawa. One of those diplomats met me and my family to help with the first days. After that, I had only one goal in mind—to find a job.

Universities in Canada had a very long process for job applications, and while I wanted to end up with a university, I needed a permanent job to sustain my family. My first 12 months were working part-time in various places and offering private mathematics lessons. I could not find a permanent teaching or research position at a university, simply because I stopped looking. I had been offered a position at Best Buy, which involved sales and performance analytics. I was engrossed by this position and by the new challenges it offered.

At that time, I began to think that I would be better off building a business career. I quit Best Buy and accepted a more complex management position at Wal-Mart. Wal-Mart offered much more complicated problems to solve, and I loved solving them. I was interested, especially in business and financial risk management. This led to a lot of work and study of this area and resulted in obtaining a financial designation – Partner Relationship Management (PRM).

However, I began to long for my academic and teaching days. I grew confident that teaching - and not pure business - was my calling. I missed teaching and working with students. The initial years of excitement working with business reports were over. This led to my renewed attempts to look for academic jobs. But this time, I began to focus on business schools since my scientific background was now mixed with a lot of business and finance knowledge. I began to teach at several colleges and universities. I also obtained an M.Ed Degree from York University to understand students' psychology better. All this led to me accepting a full-time professor position at Seneca College Business School, which I currently occupy.

Two factors had the biggest impact on my decisions leading up to this point. The first; my need to earn money to sustain myself and my family. That defined my actions. I could not obtain an academic job right away since these jobs involved a long wait for available positions and a long process. I had to accept jobs which, at that time, were alien to me. However, after some time, I began to understand business more and more, which led me to being at home at business jobs and even led to building a business career. Sometimes I did not apply to positions correctly, sometimes being viewed as being overqualified or mentioning irrelevant things on my resume or during interviews. This led to some time wasted and positions lost in the beginning. I also did not look at certain jobs based on my assumptions about them. But eventually, I learned how things worked and ended up making better decisions.

I have changed since moving to Canada. I now appreciate the stability and calmness. My behaviours are directed towards enjoying and valuing my teaching job and spending quality time with my family. I appreciate Canadian nature and developed a love for hiking and kayaking.

Advice to prospective new Canadians

My major advice would be to keep a positive attitude. Many people I knew became despondent and negative because of difficulties they faced in their first few years in Canada.

Another piece of advice I would give is to keep fighting for the goal you have in mind. A lot of people become so absorbed by everyday life that they lose track of that. No matter how difficult and time consuming the present becomes, one must always find ways to set the foundation needed.

Make sure to check on your assumptions and beliefs. They define actions, and if your assumptions are incorrect, the actions won't lead to where you want to go. It is always important to verify for oneself any rumour or any information before acting on it. The final lesson would be to be mindful of oneself and one's non-professional life in Canada.

Don't ignore what is going on around you. It will reinforce the positive attitude and professional goals in unpredictable and amazing ways! The world could definitely benefit from Canada.

MAKSIM SOKOLOV

is a professor, mathematician and business professional, specializing in quantitative performance management, risk measurement, and pricing of financial instruments.

Canada Gave me the Gift of Openness

Anonymous

Saudi Arabia

I grew up in an upper middle-class, well-educated family in Saudi Arabia. My parents valued education so much that they ensured that we went to the top-rated private schools in the country. In general, my teenage years were good. I had a lot of freedom compared to other girls my age. I went out whenever I wanted and didn't have a curfew. I could watch anything on TV and use the internet. This was surprising, even to our expat neighbours. My father wanted me to be mature, so he gave me a lot of responsibilities and held me accountable for them at a young age. Reading was an important part of our life, so my parents expected me to read books.

With all the freedom I had, I still experienced a great deal of pressure from my peers, teachers, and extended family, which created a lot of internal conflict.

My first 12 months in Canada were both fun and challenging. It was fun as it was my first time alone and it was very exciting to discover things and understand the Canadian culture. However, because of the environment I grew up in, I was not street smart so that lead to some issues.

Canada is very diverse in terms of culture, and I had to learn about different cultures and how to interact with people. My English was only conversational, and this made it exceedingly difficult to do many things such as get the right phone plan, open a bank account, and get an apartment. It was very hard to understand directions as Canadians like to use north, south, west, and east when they give directions, use transportation, or go places.

"I have friends from different faiths and cultures which is something that is specific to Canada."

In terms of school, it was challenging to focus while adapting to my new life, and the Canadian education style of teaching was completely different than how things were back home.

I had never paid any bills before coming to Canada, so I had to learn about spending and saving money.

I have friends from different faiths and cultures which is something that is specific to Canada. It encourages others to bring their beliefs and values with them. This made me less biased and provided me with insights on others and why they do things the way they do.

Fully adjusting to Canada took a long time. The feeling of belonging was hard to achieve quickly.

I describe my life in Canada to family and friends as hard but fulfilling. Stability and security are achievable in Saudi Arabia. However, it's difficult to achieve these in Canada. There is constant change, and you must adapt and have back-up plans, especially if you are on your own.

- Since coming to Canada, I have become a better person. I give credit to five learned principles:
- Tolerance: It's very important to accept others and learn about different cultures.
- Reflection: Navigating the immigration process alone allowed me to spend time reflecting on many things such as beliefs, values, and actions which made me very empathetic.
- Appreciation: All cultures are beautiful and interesting.
- Consideration and Kindness: Things work out better when I'm nice and kind to others, without being a pushover. No problem can be solved with anger, and no one wants to help if I appear angry and entitled.
- Accountability: It's important to take responsibility for my mistakes.

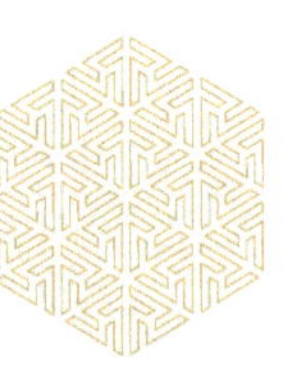

Advice to prospective new Canadians

If I could share wisdom with those that are walking down the same road, I would tell them that if you felt or act like an outsider you will never fit in. It's very important to believe that you are now part of the fabric of this country as it will make things a lot easier. Otherwise, you will create a barrier for people to break through. It's important to remember that as an immigrant, you are starting from zero, therefore, use time wisely and spend it helping to establish yourself and becoming independent. Consider every opportunity that comes your way no matter how small it is; it will always lead to something better. Take advantage of the programs that the government offers for immigrants and Canadians. Know your rights or at least pretend to know them so no one takes advantage of you. Finally, do not resist change. Priorities, values, and beliefs will transition with time as you meet new people and become exposed to different environments. Change is beautiful. Embrace it.

I Found a Home away from Home

Zaheed Alibhai

United Kingdom

People migrate from one place to another for different reasons. For me, the decision to move to Canada from the U.K. suddenly grew stronger after I married my Canadian wife, Salha. Although I had a great career as a tax consultant at Deloitte, it gradually dawned on me that my future didn't lie in the U.K. Let's just say despite being British, I have never felt "British enough" due to my background and the color of my skin. My Muslim parents had immigrated into the U.K. in the 1970s, a time when there was outright discrimination and blatant racism. Fortunately, I went through my secondary and university education in the 1990s, when multiculturalism was highly celebrated in the U.K. However, this euphoria didn't last for too long as the 9/11 and 7/7 incidents in New York City and London, respectively, gave way to a rise in racial profiling. Of course, all the anti-Muslim sentiments at the time brought a sense of uneasiness to me.

Canada was easily a natural choice for me since I have never quite felt like a "full-fledged Brit"

Canada wasn't an entirely new place as I had visited my extended family there several times. Although I didn't initially plan to relocate there, I later came to the realization that Canada was a practical place to raise a family. Moreover, even though Canada was in many ways an extension of the U.K. and part of the Commonwealth, it was a young nation that accommodated people

"My first year in Canada was simply one of transition, as I faced some difficulties settling and getting accustomed to my new environment."

from different parts of the world, irrespective of their backgrounds. There was also the beautiful infrastructural factor, coupled with the fact that wanderlust was in my blood since my parents were also immigrants in the U.K.

The process of moving to Canada wasn't complicated for me as I was fortunate to work with Deloitte, an organization that promotes global mobility. My initial move to Canada in 2011 was therefore via a work permit processed through Deloitte. Having planned with my wife to make Canada our home, I later applied for a resident permit, which was again facilitated by my employer. Thankfully, I had two grounds to apply for a resident permit: I had worked in Canada for a qualifying period; and, moreover, my spouse was Canadian.

My first year in Canada was simply one of transition, as I faced some difficulties settling and getting accustomed to my new environment. A major challenge I encountered was adapting to the long winter, which is characterized by extreme cold temperatures.

"Canadians have a balanced worldview."

Luckily for me, the right infrastructure was in place to deal with such harsh weather. I didn't like the sedentary lifestyle in Canada and besides, it also took me a while to get accustomed to driving on the other side of the road. However, my wife, Salha, whom I consider having had the biggest impact on my life in Canada, was there to guide me through all these challenges. I also had amazing colleagues who were always ready to help.

Within five years, I had become a fulfilled man with a beautiful wife, a blossoming career and two kids. The birth of my two sons, Qais and Zayn in 2013 and 2014, respectively, remains a highlight of my life in Canada. My wife and I also purchased a home and even though we were quite busy at work, I would make time occasionally and travel with my family to experience other Canadian cities like: Vancouver, BC; Calgary, AB; Halifax, NS; and Montreal, QC. At this point, I was impressed by the fact that the Canadian system afforded me an opportunity to strike a balance between work and family life.

In 2015, my family had an opportunity to move to Dubai, where we would live for the next three and a half years. I had been contacted by a competing company and offered an attractive pay package. The timing was somewhat perfect for us given the age of our children and a huge bonus of the year-round warm weather. My wife and I had always dreamt of also experiencing life in the Middle East. The offer was therefore quite tempting as we imagined the beautiful climate, great halal food, and the fact that Dubai was a more accommodating place where we could easily get help with the kids. As I continued my life in Dubai, one thing that struck me was the fact that whenever I was asked where I was from, I would hastily say "from Canada", despite having a British passport.

Well, we had always wanted our children to grow up in Canada and benefit from the Canadian education system. So, as the kids approached the kindergarten age, we made the decision to return to our home in Canada in February 2019. Of course, it was tough adjusting to the 50 degrees temperature shift between the two continents, but we successfully settled in again. It was once more awesome to be back in Toronto and with my former employer.

Having experienced the Canadian lifestyle, I can describe Canada as a place of balance and diversity. Canadians have a balanced worldview and uphold the equality of all, irrespective of race or creed. This upstanding value of the respect of human rights makes me proud to call Canada my home.

Advice to prospective new Canadians

I always advise people planning to immigrate to Canada be aware of the numerous challenges. The truth is that although welcoming, the country equally has strict immigration policies that must be followed by all aspiring immigrants. Even though these modalities might be stringent, it is a meticulous process that allows individuals to live in a vibrant and harmonious society. Rest assured that once you successfully settle in, Canada will easily become your favorite country.

ZAHEED ALIBHAI

is a partner at a global professional services firm, a British national and Canadian permanent resident of South Asian heritage.

Same Language... Different Culture

Mary Kilmer-Tchalekian

United States of America

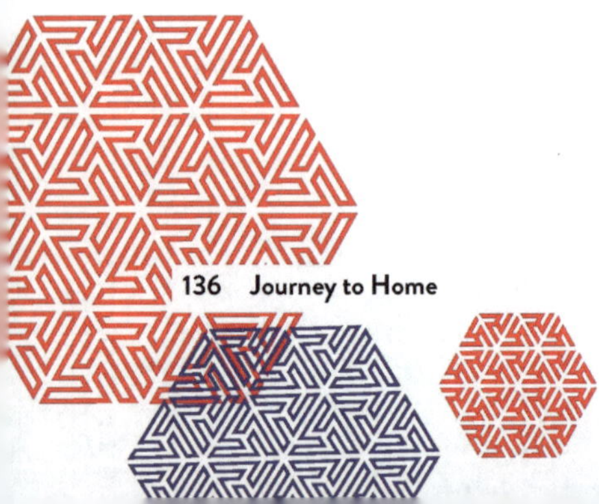

Canada became my home when as a newlywed I moved to Victoria, B.C in December 1972. My husband had been living and teaching there, at Royal Roads Military College (now Royal Roads University). Thus, moving to Canada was part of the package of getting married and settling into married life. My husband, Chavarche Tchalekian, was born in Helwan, Egypt, and was educated both there and in the U.S. He had become a Canadian citizen a few short months before we married.

At the time of my coming to Canada, I had finished all course work for my doctorate in Spanish from the University of Texas in Austin, Texas and was working on my doctoral dissertation. I completed it in 1974.

My husband had already started the application process for my landed immigrant status before I left Texas, so virtually all I had to do when I arrived was complete an interview with an immigration officer in Victoria. It was quite simple at that time, unlike the far more complex process today.

Getting acquainted with my new surroundings in Victoria and meeting Chavarche's colleagues at Royal Roads and other friends of his while working on my dissertation were my main activities during my first year in Canada. While there were some cultural differences between life in Canada and life in the U.S., but these were relatively easy to adjust to. I had previously spent a year studying in Spain and another

"We have not yet fully embraced the Indigenous peoples or learned to value Indigenous cultures as much as we should."

year as a Fulbright scholar in Colombia, so I was somewhat acquainted with what living in a different cultural realm entailed, but challenges of this nature were very few in my transition to life in Canada. Clearly, learning a new language and mastering it was not one of the challenges I faced.

In my first five years here in Canada I became a mother to our son Antranik, taught Spanish language and literature at the University of Victoria, and settled more fully into the life and lifestyle of Victoria through frequent visits with friends and new acquaintances. Being far from my family in New York State was probably the biggest challenge I faced those first few years. But this pales in comparison to what many immigrants face when distances from family and friends are even greater.

My work in the International Division of Niagara College Canada has, without a doubt, had the greatest and most long-lasting impact on me as a person and on my life in Canada. If Jos Nolle, my former boss and director of the International Division, had not recognized my skills and potential and offered me a

"Canada has taught me to be more respectful, to value diversity, and to refrain from making hasty value judgements."

position on the International Projects team, I would not have lived as fulfilling and rewarding a life as I have in the past 25 years. I am infinitely grateful to Jos for mentoring me and introducing me to the values of working on an international scale. My work with other colleagues and students at Niagara College, as well as with Latin American educators provided untold challenges and rewards.

I must credit my son Antranik, who works with The Arthritis Society in Toronto, with having had a totally different but enduring impact on me. He has often been my window into the arts and creative processes. Additionally, he has kept me abreast of the music scene throughout the years. He has kept me connected with the younger generation, which continues to keep me young and energetic.

When friends or family ask about Canada or comment on it, I tell them that Canadians are by and large respectful of others, certainly more inclusive than people are in other parts of the world, and far more courteous than people in the U.S., for example. However, I feel that we have not yet fully embraced the Indigenous peoples or learned to value Indigenous cultures as much as we should, although we are working on it. I also comment on the relative degree of peaceful and law-abiding citizens that I have found here. I say that that I don't mind paying taxes because I recognize the benefits that we derive from them. Many people comment on how well-organized things are here, how clean, and prosperous towns and villages and cities are, and I agree. I also opine that we all must work harder at living peacefully together, and endeavor to reduce the effects of climate change. We can do so much more when we work together. Bono is right: the world needs more Canada.

Canada has taught me to be more respectful, to value diversity, and to refrain from making hasty value judgements. This came more acutely into focus when I was completing international project work and teaching an International Communications and Protocol course at Niagara College. When we communicate well and meaningfully, we do not have to resort to loud voices and guns.

Advice to prospective new Canadians

Meet Canadians; don't reduce your circle to living among people of the same culture as that from where you came. Be prepared to embrace change.

MARY KILMER- TCHALEKIAN

has devoted most of her professional life to education and collaborating productively with others, particularly international educators. Mary now mainly gardens, dances, and composes songs.

It Wasn't Easy, But It Was Worth It

Marta Rzeszowska Chavent, Alina & Wladyslaw Rzeszowski

Poland

I was born in Krakow, Poland, which was a communist state in the 1980s. The impact of this political landscape was much less significant on me (as a child) than it was on my parents, who had limited liberty due to the political system that was in place. My childhood memories include walking into grocery stores where shelves were lined with empty bottles and little, if any, produce or products. I have vivid memories of waiting in line for several hours for an allotted bag of oranges, only to find out that the supply had run out by the time we got to the front of the line. The wait felt long—and cold in the middle of a frigid winter. I didn't understand the full implications of the political system until I was much older. My life before moving to Canada revolved around a large extended family and the comfort of a small but cozy apartment outside of Krakow, which our tribe of three called home.

My father made the brave and bold decision to leave Poland, eventually coming to Canada via a stop in Austria. My mother and I waited two years as he navigated his and our immigration status amidst administrative processes that I was too young to understand or appreciate. We were able to join my father in Toronto, Ontario in 1984, during one of the coldest winters on record. The Canadian government had extended an invitation to immigrants who were willing to engage in manual labour. My father made the decision to take this offer to exit the communist system, not having fully appreciated how far or cold Canada would be from the familiarity of Europe and Poland in particular.

"My parent's perseverance has had the biggest impact on my life here."

Our arrival to Canada was filled with its own share of struggles, of which my parents bore the burden. This included a long period of separation, where our only contact with my father was via a monthly scheduled call that we would book at the local post office. We eventually had a phone line installed in our apartment, which helped us stay connected while he was abroad and trying to secure our arrival to Canada. With no English language skills or any local contacts and a basic grade school education that taught him survival skills, my father was in for quite the shock when he landed at the airport, with only a few dollar bills in his pocket. Luckily, he stumbled upon a Polish community in Toronto, which provided moral and logistical support in navigating daily life and the permanent resident process. He held many menial jobs (two or three at a time was the norm) as did most immigrants back then (and many still do today), as he saved up money to secure a place for us to live. In the winter of 1983, my father joined nine other Polish men on a hunger strike in front of the

Polish Embassy in Toronto to raise awareness for their administrative struggles. All ten men were looking to sponsor their families who were unable to freely leave communist Poland and join their spouses and fathers in Canada. The hunger strike lasted almost three weeks and yielded the desired results after garnering much media, political, and public support. As a result, my mother and I were able to reunite with my father a few months later and the same held true for the others involved. Many years later a documentary was made of this historic event, entitled Ten Hungry Men. I was so proud to accompany my dad to the screening event, and once again humbled by the sacrifice he and the others had made to provide the next generation with a fruitful future.

Back in those early days, as a second grader who didn't speak a word of English and had no exposure to life outside of my family home, I was completely overwhelmed in, and by, Canada. The winter was too cold, the people spoke too quickly, the stores were too full of things. I hated the change and everything around me and I made this known to my parents daily. I cried every night and begged to go back "home". My parents finally succumbed to my begging and sent me back to Poland for summer vacations during the first few years.

Eventually I grew accustomed to the cold winters and every other season. Once I learned English, I began to embrace the change and became empathetic to the struggle of other new immigrants that arrived after me. Canada eventually started to feel like home by the third year and I no longer needed to spend my summers back in Poland. I now felt at home in Canada and was able to navigate this new life that I began to appreciate incrementally, year over year.

Language was one of the biggest challenges, for both myself and my parents. Since I was able to pick up English much faster than my parents, I became their official translator. I clearly remember accompanying my parents to the bank to negotiate their first mortgage with a mixture of pride and anxiety. It's not something most ten-year-old kids did at the time, but it became the norm in our family. I reviewed invoices, typed up rental agreements and called the utilities company when there was a billing error. I often resented this additional responsibility, especially when the teen years came along, but I also took pride years later, knowing that I had made an important contribution to our tight-knit clan. My parents worked hard, and I knew not to take that for granted. Immigrant kids had to grow up faster in many ways.

My parent's perseverance has had the biggest impact on my life here. My father's positive outlook, even when the odds were stacked against him, has always been admirable, as has my mother's unwavering support. I suppose

> **"Language was one of the biggest challenges"**

their characters wouldn't have been any different had we stayed in Poland. Perhaps the immigrant mentality honed their survival skills.

In the early days, when I would visit Poland during my summer vacation, my description of Canada to friends and relatives wasn't very inspiring, but as the years went on my perspective changed. I eventually ended up visiting Poland less frequently as I started to enjoy attending Canadian summer camps. I would describe Canada as an immensely welcoming place, where I had the opportunity to interact with people from a myriad of countries and cultures. I took pride in tasting the local dishes that my diverse friends exposed me to via their own home cooking. I became an unabashed ambassador for the diversity that Canada represents.

Watching my parents succeed without language skills or close access to extended family has honed my own perseverance and desire to explore the world (perhaps not what they hoped for) and in turn I have visited and lived in many countries, as a student and adult. I have also found great pride in mentoring new immigrants, as I can fully appreciate the struggle of settling down and looking for meaningful work and the eventual benefits that come with navigating, and eventually thriving, in a new country, culture, and community.

I would tell those that wish to immigrate to come with realistic expectations, wherever you go. As much as Canada is a welcoming place and there is now a myriad of support services available to new Canadians, there are still going to be roadblocks. Having the patience and perseverance to overcome them is key. Find a support system, dedicate time early on to learn English fluently (this is something my parents regret not doing early on, as they were too busy working multiple jobs to attend the free ESL classes that were provided).

There is so much good in Canada and in Canadians. Of course, we have more work to do, (for example, welcoming new Canadians by embracing their professional designations), but the country and people have a lot to offer. Immigrants have contributed extensively to the fabric of Canada and anyone who is seriously thinking of immigrating to another country likely already possesses the spirit of hard work, ingenuity, and bravery that such a life decision necessitates.

I would also advise others to do their research (which is much easier to access now than it was in the 1980s) and get connected to a community. It doesn't have to be a culturally identical group. You can create community through a sport you like, an instrument you play, your profession or passion. Do everything you can to meet others early on to avoid isolation and to learn from their experiences.

I dedicate this story to my father, Wladyslaw, and am forever grateful for the sacrifices that he and my mom made by coming to Canada. I have certainly benefited from their perseverance and together we lamented, laughed, learned, and led each other on this immigrant journey. I remain immensely grateful to my mom and dad for their unwavering support and incredibly brave decision to move to Canada.

Advice to prospective new Canadians

Meet Canadians; don't reduce your circle to living among people of the same culture as that from where you came. Be prepared to embrace change.

MARTA CHAVENT

resides in France with her husband and children and continues to consider Canada her home. She remains immensely grateful to her dad for making the brave decision to move to Canada and to her mom for her unwavering support.

An Educated Journey

Veronica Costea

Romania

"One of the things that really helped me through the winter was the Toronto Public Library."

I was born and raised in a small town in northwestern region of Romania (a region known to many as Transylvania). I had a very sheltered childhood even though I was born at a time when Romania was under communist dictatorship, of which I truly learned only afterwards. I was seven years old when communism fell and the long transition to democracy began. My parents are both engineers, but both ended up pursuing careers in education, my mother as a high school teacher, and my father as a university lecturer. I grew up loving books and languages. I was fortunate to have many opportunities to study abroad, first in Dublin, Ireland; then Paris, France; and then in Kobe, Japan. These experiences opened me up to the world and really broadened my mind. In 2003, I married my high school sweetheart, and our son was born in 2006 just as I was completing my master's degree in Irish Cultural Studies, after a BA in English and Japanese. After one year on maternity leave, I started a PhD in Literature, while working as a teaching and research assistant at the Babes Bolyai University in Cluj-Napoca, Romania. My husband had also graduated with a master's degree and had fulfilled his dream of becoming a high school teacher. I led a fairly privileged life back home prior to moving to Canada. I had access to great education, a loving family, and great friends. But at the time Romania was still going through the long post-communist transition and once we graduated and started our family it became obvious that it would be very hard to make a living on our teaching salaries, although we both loved our jobs and got a great sense of fulfillment from them. I was also embarking on a research career and was starting to feel the limitations of doing so in a place where access to latest information and resources in any field was extremely problematic.

There was a combination of factors that led to our decision to move to Canada.

On the one hand, we were feeling a little bit stuck. In a sense, both my husband and I had achieved our career goals in that we were fortunate to be doing the jobs we had dreamed of. However, once our son was born, reality hit us hard as we realized that we were struggling to support ourselves on our salaries, without any real perspective that things would change soon. We were both doing jobs we loved, but we were really struggling to make ends meet.

On the other hand, both of us suffer from some chronic form of wanderlust and have always had difficulty being in one place for too long. We just love exploring new things and, in

"I was amazed at the visible diversity of people. It felt like anyone could be at home here."

a sense, it was a new adventure, an opportunity to meet new people, have new experiences, and grow as individuals through these experiences.

The trigger for our decision was a visit from one of our friends who had moved to Canada a few years before. As we learned from our friend about his family's experience, my husband became more and more enthusiastic about giving this a shot. Since he had followed me to Japan a few years earlier on a similar adventure, and our son was young, and we were just beginning to feel the burden of our responsibility as parents, we decided to try applying for permanent residency in Canada under the Federal Skilled Workers Program.

We applied for permanent residency under the Skilled Workers Program in early 2007. We were expecting the process to take about three years, but our visas came through in the fall of 2008. We then took a few months to wrap things up back home and sell our apartment and eventually landed in April 2009. Things went extremely smoothly as we both had higher education degrees and were proficient in both English and French, so our application went through without a problem. The hard part was saying good-bye to our friends and family and facing the unknown, just the three of us.

We had decided that for the first three months we would come without our son. We left him with my mother back home. We were thinking that it would probably be best to first find a place to live, get some furniture, and figure out all the administrative things like getting a driver's license and a healthcare card. He was not yet three years old at the time and leaving him behind for three months was one of the hardest decisions I have ever made. In hindsight, it was the right decision.

One of my first impressions was that, compared to all other places I had lived before, it seemed to be so easy to fit in. I was amazed at the visible diversity of people. It felt like anyone could be at home here. I was so excited at the prospect of meeting people from all around the world. It was also a beautiful spring and, although I was genuinely shocked at how cold the wind was in early April, I remember taking long walks around our new neighborhood with magnolias in bloom. It felt like a world of possibilities had opened. We were lucky to have some friends and family here and I think that made all the difference, because from the very beginning it truly felt like a place, we could call home in time.

Of course, not everything was all rosy in the beginning. There were a lot of things that were harder than we had anticipated.

My husband had been promised a job in construction by our friend and he started working soon after we first arrived. Little did we know that working for $10/hour (which sounded like a generous amount while we were still back home) could hardly sustain our family. We supplemented that income as I kept some of my clients for whom I had done freelance translation work back in Romania. But they were paying me the same rates as before, while the cost of living was tenfold here in Canada. I was lucky enough to get a full-time job for an American translation agency working remotely as an editor and, after about six months, my husband also managed to find another job in a call centre where they were looking for bilingual people. He had a definite advantage being fluent in four languages.

Our son also struggled in the beginning. He started talking very early and his vocabulary in Romanian was strong at this point. He was a chatterbox and would just start talking to anyone who would listen. So, coming here and being faced with the language barrier, the fact that he could not understand other children and they could not understand him was very tough. We noticed that whereas before he was a very easygoing and friendly child, who had no problem sharing his toys and who made friends instantly, he was now becoming aggressive with other children. I remember so vividly when I once asked him why he was so upset with another child at the park and he told me, sobbing, "Because he doesn't hear me!" We decided to enroll him in a playgroup at a community centre nearby, thinking that would help him pick up the language. The first few weeks were heartbreaking. He would cry inconsolably for the two hours that he was there, four days a week. Then one day, I got a call from the teacher. I picked up as I was thinking that's it, they are calling me to pick him up, they must have given up. Instead, they had called to tell me that Bogdan was having a great day. "He is playing with the other kids and having fun, and, by the way, he also speaks quite fluent English!" To me it felt like a small miracle. Until then, I had barely heard him say anything in English beyond "Hello" and "Thank you" and "Goodbye" and suddenly, his English was as good as all the other children in the group. I think, in addition to the lovely teachers who were so immensely patient, we probably also have Thomas the Tank Engine and Dora the Explorer to thank for that.

As for myself, I remember the first summer as one spent discovering so many new things and beautiful places around the city. But I also worried a lot about how things would work out. I had hoped that I would be able to get a job as a teacher but was completely discouraged by what seemed to be a lengthy and costly process. I had spent 20 years of my life in school by then and felt it was completely unfair to have been accepted as a permanent resident under the Skilled Workers Program, where my education had secured us such a high score, only to find out that pretty much all my degrees were essentially worthless here without a lengthy process of assessment and going back to school. It was also discouraging to find myself caught in a vicious cycle of not being able to get a job without finding a spot for my son in childcare, yet not being able afford to put my child in childcare without having a job.

However, I was fortunate enough to be able to tap into my language skills and ended up with a contract with an American translation company, working as editor 30 hours a week from home. That was a real blessing as it allowed me to be with my son as he was still adjusting to his new environment while also starting to build experience and earn an income.

One of the things I remember most vividly is our first winter here. It wasn't just the cold and the wind, but an overwhelming feeling of being trapped and powerless. The Ministry of Transportation had gone on strike before I had gotten a chance to get my G2 license, and it lasted all through the winter, for seven long months. We were living in an area very poorly serviced by public transit, so with a young child and a car in the garage that I was not allowed to drive, going anywhere was extremely challenging.

One of the things that really helped me through the winter was the Toronto Public Library. I could not believe what a wonderful system this was being able to search books online, place them on hold, and pick them up from our local branch, knowing that pretty much any book I could possibly want, the library would have. There were also free events that were within reach through the library. I remember seeing some of my favorite writers in person during that time and it felt almost like I was living someone else's life. I could hardly believe it was so easy to go and listen to people like Salman Rushdie speak.

Most importantly though, we had connected with several families, all newcomers like us, and became friends. I was so touched by the solidarity that seemed to emerge between these people so naturally, all from far away and trying to build a life in Canada, coming together and helping each other. We watched each other's children, shared information as we were learning new things, helped each other put together resumes. We were there to share our challenges, frustrations, dreams, and hopes.

During our first five years, our son started kindergarten and then school in a French immersion program. It became gradually obvious that to him this was home, even as we were still feeling a bit foreign to this new land. We started a routine that I believe many immigrants share, of sending him back home to Romania every summer. With very little family here we truly wanted to make sure that he got to know his family, that he kept his native language alive and that he continued to be connected to our roots. My husband changed a few jobs until he found something that he truly enjoyed and by the 5th anniversary of our arrival in Canada he had been promoted to manager.

I was able to go back to school and complete a certificate in community interpreting. I had worked as a conference interpreter back home, but community interpreting was a whole new world to discover. Working from home as an editor, while very convenient, was at the same time very lonely. I was longing to interact more with people and thought blending work as a translator and editor with community interpreting would be a great solution. I also got certified as a translator which opened more opportunities. And all this in the end led me to MCIS Language Solutions, a non-profit organization providing translation and interpretation services to mediate access to critical information and services to newcomers facing language barriers. I started there as a volunteer in 2011. Shortly after I was offered a full-time job as a translation coordinator and then was promoted to supervisor.

At that point, quite unexpectedly, I was offered an opportunity to apply for a research grant in Japan. Since I had interrupted my PhD studies when we had moved to Canada, I think I had some underlying regrets related to having abandoned my academic career. I had hoped to be able to pursue that in Canada, but in the beginning, it just did not work out and as time

"I have become more open-minded and humbler by living in Canada."

went by it felt that it would become harder and harder to enter that world here. So, I decided to take this opportunity, applied, and was awarded the 18-month grant. I went. My son remained in Canada with my husband for the first three months. I came back for him, and he spent the next three months with me in Akita, Japan. It turned out that adjusting to life in Japan was very difficult for him. He was just starting Grade 1 at the time and the culture shock was huge, not to mention the communication difficulties. The program itself was a bit of a disappointment to me and the experience helped me realize that in fact I had no real desire to return to academia. I had found a career much better suited to me working in the non-profit sector in Canada, using my skills to help refugees and immigrants, so we came back after six months.

I think that perhaps that return from Japan marked a symbolic milestone for me, as it truly felt like a homecoming. Another milestone was the day we received our Canadian citizenship, shortly after, so that we could now officially call ourselves Canadian.

In those first five years we also built our family away from home—good friends to share all our special moments with. We discovered the great outdoors and found a renewed love of camping.

We never miss an opportunity to take off for a long weekend, exploring the gorgeous scenery.

While in general I think our transition to our life in Canada was very smooth, there were of course inevitable challenges, some of which I have mentioned above.

I think the one major challenge was around employment—finding jobs that matched our skills without any previous "Canadian Experience," and balancing our family life with very busy professional lives.

There have been countless people who have made our transition to our new life in Canada possible, easy, and fun, and I am deeply grateful to all of them. However, if I am to choose one answer only, it would have to be MCIS, the organization I continue to work for and the people I work with. It is a place where I have found a lot of support and have been offered tremendous opportunities to learn and grow, but most importantly, to find a purpose. I had always been fascinated by and drawn to languages. I have a degree in languages. I had worked as a language teacher and as a linguistic researcher. But at MCIS I found a place where I could contribute all this to a purpose higher than myself. I go to work knowing that I do what I love, but also, more importantly, that we are making a difference in people's lives. I work with people from all around the world who are like family to me. I am also offered a lot of space to be creative and to continue to learn. While there are challenges of course, I genuinely feel that at MCIS I can be the best version of myself and pay forward all the support I have received as an immigrant by helping other immigrants and refugees.

When speaking about Canada, we talk a lot about the long winters and the cold, and the wind. I also think many people think we are exaggerating until they get here. I also always talk about the vast spaces, about how everything seems so small every time I return to Europe. I often mention the great diversity and how amazing it is to be able to get a taste of every culture on this planet within one city. It's all in the little details. We share our small victories, our big achievements, our setbacks, our joys, and our moments of sadness, but mostly I say that Canada is truly a place of possibilities. I feel like I can do anything if I set my mind to it.

I have become more open-minded and humbler by living in Canada. I have learned that there is a diversity of ways in which you can look at anything, that our opinions, views, and ideas are never the only way. So, I truly see the world in a very different way.

The last 10 years have truly been a great adventure. I have learned a lot about myself and about the world in the process. Perhaps the most important thing though is that each one of us truly have the strength and the skills to reinvent ourselves.

I believe the world does need more tolerance,

openness to diversity, kindness, understanding, and more respect for human rights. I think it is also always important to not lose sight of the issues Canada does have. As Canadians we should always strive to make Canada even better.

On a practical note, I would tell those who are thinking of coming here that information is key. I think anyone planning to move to Canada should try to prepare by gathering as much information as possible. There are a lot of misconceptions among newcomers about how things work in Canada. So, my advice is to get information from as wide a range of sources as possible: talk to people you know who have come to Canada; explore online forums; look at online resources. Do not blindly act on information that comes from one person only. We all have our different experiences and what works for one person might not work for you.

Once in Canada I recommend accessing the settlement services available to all newcomers. One of the best things we have done in our early days in Canada was go to an employment centre where we enrolled in a series of workshops on building a resume, doing job interviews, and so on. To this day, 10 years later, I find the information I got through that workshop extremely useful, and I think it played a huge part in finding jobs and advancing our careers quickly in our new home.

Advice to prospective new Canadians

I often see newcomers struggling and sometimes the services they need are right there, but they do not know they are available. A settlement agency can play a huge role in pointing people in the right direction, whether it's for housing, healthcare, education, training, employment, childcare, or recreation.

VERONICA COSTEA

has worked in the language industry for 17 years as a translator, interpreter, language teacher, and in computational linguistics research. Currently, her work involves managing the delivery of language services. Her focus is assisting immigrants and refugees facing language barriers in accessing critical information and services. Veronica lives in Toronto, Ontario.

From Privilege to Responsibility

Varinder Gill

India

I had a very comfortable life before coming to Canada. I completed my master's degree at the age of 22 and started with my PhD. At the same time, I got a full-time job in a college that was funded by the government. My social life was quite healthy as I had all my siblings, cousin brothers, and sisters in India. After my marriage, I continued with the job and was able to maintain my social life as I visited my parents quite frequently. My husband was a full-time employee with a bank. As we had decent amount of cash flow, we were able to afford servants to take care of the household chores such as laundry, cleaning, and washing dishes, so I had more time for other things such as investing time in my kids, studying for my PhD, among other academic activities. I had my own house, car, was financially independent and lived a comfortable life. My son attended a private school for a better education as the quality of education in government schools was extremely poor.

Canada is a country where immigration is easy for skilled workers. It is receptive to new immigrants and provides initial support for newcomers. My husband did intensive online research about Canada, life in Canada for newcomers, rules, regulations, and potential job opportunities. We also had discussions about moving to Canada with our distant relatives and friends living here, as we wanted to gather more information about their experiences here and pros and cons of leaving to immigrate.

"You cannot come here without sacrificing your comfort level. Once you survive these challenging times, you will have a better life here."

Filling the complete permanent residence application was a very tedious process. Arranging all the supporting documents was quite overwhelming for us due to time constraints with our jobs. Once we applied for immigration, it took eight years to receive communication about getting our medicals. My daughter was born seven years after applying for PR, so it took us even longer due to the addition in our family.

The first year was not an easy time for us. My husband resigned from his job in India before moving to Canada, whereas I took a leave from my college for one month. The initial month was quite disappointing for us as everything was new, such as driving rules, traffic rules, written and verbal communication, and people's way of interacting. We stayed with our distant relatives for one month, and that made everything a little easier as they were quite supportive and guided us through life here in Canada. My husband started visiting employment agencies

"The most important behavioral change for me was becoming more responsible."

and applying for jobs in different banks. He is a quick learner, so he learned about different routes and transit services. He used to spend his whole day visiting agencies, working on his resume, and talking to other people. He got a job at the Royal Bank of Canada (RBC) as a full-time employee after one month. I went back to India and re-joined my job. My resigning from the job was a big decision for me as it was a full-time unionized position. I stayed in India for eight months with my kids, and my husband moved into a small apartment. Those eight months were not easy for us as we were not able to decide if I should resign. Finally, we decided to burn all bridges and I quit. When I arrived here and stayed in a small space, it was very disappointing for me. Moving from a big house to an apartment was difficult, though my husband and kids were able to manage.

The first five years here were challenging as I was emotionally connected to my siblings in India, and I had to miss all the social gatherings. I was quite unhappy about that. I did not have a job for the first year which was quite painful as the feeling of being unemployed and not earning anything was unpleasant. We did not ask for any financial support from our parents. I did not get a chance to visit India during the first five years. When I got job here in Canada, my kids started going to a babysitter that my son did not like at all. My mother visited us after four years and stayed with us for a few months. Those months were quite relaxing as she helped me with household chores and took care of my kids.

We didn't buy a car for first two years so one of the biggest challenges was travelling on buses, especially with my small kids. Transit is quite expensive for a newcomer. Looking for a job was another big challenge. I started visiting different employment agencies, attended workshops on building my resume, and visited different organizations to gather information about bridging programs. All these activities were painful for me as I was suddenly unemployed after having a respectable full-time job for 10 years in India earning a decent salary. My husband was always supportive, and he never wanted me to settle for any job. I started networking with people in different banks and requested to meet the bank manager. I remember my visit to one bank, where the customer service representative wanted to know why I wanted to speak to the bank manager. The moment I said I wanted to drop off my resume, his attitude changed, and said the manager was busy and that he would forward my resume.

Also, general advice from people, friends, and relatives around me was difficult to accept, especially when they advised that I should look for an entry level positions. They said that it would be impossible to get a job in a college as professor as there was nothing in this sector and the employers prefer people with Canadian credentials and experience.

The biggest impact on my life was the positive attitude of people that I met in different colleges and universities here. When I was new, I started contacting people in the education sector requesting information about how colleges work here in Canada. Most of them had a welcoming response and they agreed to meet and help with my resume and show me how to build network. They connected me to other people. One of them offered me a project developing an outline for a course. This is how I started my professional journey. Another person invited me to attend her class so that I could understand the classroom dynamics and teaching methodology.

I tell friends and family that Canada is not a country for people who are not ready to explore new options, embark on new adventures or learn new things. Canada is a land of opportunity for people who push themselves beyond their limits, leave their comfort zone, and are ready to learn and persevere. I would suggest that they should give themselves at least five years to settle in Canada and be ready for struggles and a difficult transition phase. I would also tell them to be ready to face cultural and language barriers and to embrace Canadians values. You cannot come here without sacrificing your comfort level. Canada is a country where the individual's life is valued. Once you learn the rules and regulations of this country and lead your life without breaking them, you will have a peaceful and stress-free life. Also, be ready to pay higher taxes, though you will enjoy better health benefits and free education.

"Once you survive these challenging times, you will have a better life here."

The most important behavioral change for me was becoming more responsible. In India, I was not responsible enough as I had my in-laws taking care of most of the household-related work. When we moved here, we had no choice. We were careful with using resources such as water and electricity. My organization and time management skills improved as I had more household responsibilities. I have become wiser with spending money.

Advice to prospective new Canadians

Know your rights and responsibilities, be honest, and be ready to acknowledge your mistakes. You must work hard and give yourself some time to relax while going through the difficult transition phase. Do not push yourself too hard to adapt to the new environment all at a once. It will take time. Come with a positive attitude. Do not panic, as this will lead to frustration.

Canada embraces diversity and values people's lives by providing a relatively safe environment. Understand your responsibilities as a citizen and embrace diversity.

VARINDER GILL

is an educator, curriculum developer, and a researcher with a PhD in economics. She has worked at various educational institutions and is currently working as a college professor in Ontario.

A Steady Climb

Habib Meghjee

Tanzania

I was born in Mwanza, Tanzania and was 18 years old when I immigrated to Canada. My parents were also born in Africa and my grandparents were born in India. I was born into a simple family. My father had a small shop selling clothing and my mum was a housewife. We were five siblings with two elder sisters, me, and two younger brothers.

Life in Tanzania was good; there was plenty of greenery, fresh fruits, and organic food. Every day, a local farmer would knock on our door offering fresh ingredients to cook with and fresh milk and bread for the day. My father's business income was enough to cover necessities like rent, food, and basic supplies.

My father had eight brothers and three sisters, and my mother had four brothers and two sisters, many of whom lived walking distance from home or in neighboring towns. I grew up with a large extended family, many cousins, and a strong faith-based practicing community around me. There were some years in my childhood that I spent living at my uncle's house, which was closer to school. My sister lived with another uncle—despite having many children on their own. This concept of children being given to other family members to care for was common. A child belonged to the entire family and to the community as well.

Our day started very early in the morning, getting ready for school at 7a.m. Homes in Mwanza only had one bathroom. At my house

"Our cozy small-town life was very different from the fast-passed environment of our new city."

we shared one bathroom for seven people. After having some bread and butter for breakfast, I walked 20 min to school with my cousins. Most of the days, we walked back home for a fresh lunch, then back for our afternoon lessons. After school we attended madrassah (religious school) followed by congregational prayers at the mosque. Another batch of fresh food awaited us when we returned home for dinner. I spent the evenings finishing my homework, playing outside, and listening to the radio.

There was a trend that after Form IV (Grade 12), students would go abroad to study in the United Kingdom, India, or Pakistan. However, only affluent families could afford to send their children to study overseas.

My elder sister soon got married and moved to Dar-es-Salam, the capital city of Tanzania at that time. My brother in-law was an ambitious professional who was constantly looking for greener pastures beyond Tanzania. He visited Canada in 1970 and really loved the place. He convinced my sister to move to Canada and in 1975 they settled in Toronto. When my second sister wanted to study in Canada, my elder sister went to the immigration office to get some

"We looked forward to our first winter and watching the Maple Leafs play ice hockey."

information about the process of how she could assist her to come study in Canada.

The immigration officer was very nice. After listening to my elder sister and finding out a little more about our family, he advised her to sponsor my parents so we could all come under my parents' sponsorship. We completed the application forms, went through medical tests and soon we were in Toronto in August 1981. There were six of us now, and we left behind many of our family members and community friends whom we missed dearly when we arrived at our new home.

Upon arrival in Toronto, my second sister took a job to support the family as my father had suffered a stroke just a few weeks before arrival in Canada. We made ends meet with one income, living in a modest apartment building. My three brothers and I went to school. Although we knew English, we did struggle with English as a subject at school. We were not fond of writing long essays or reading complicated passages from Shakespeare's various plays.

We enjoyed being in Toronto with its tall buildings, efficient bus and subway systems, and wide roads. We took note of the grocery stores and having to store food for days instead of fresh food being delivered daily. Similarly, we observed the different dressing styles and how they didn't always correlate to one's social class. Back in Mwanza, those who dressed in ironed, classy clothes were of higher income and from more affluent families. In Toronto, casual dressing was very common and acceptable even if you were of status.

Our cozy small-town life was very different from the fast-passed environment of our new city. Often it felt our days continued to be busy into the late evenings. Meal prepping and cooking started after work and chores were completed till night.

We looked forward to our first winter and watching the Maple Leafs play ice hockey. Coming from Tanzania where football or soccer is the main sport, it took time adjusting to hockey on Saturday nights.

We slowly integrated into our society by building connections with family and friends from back home who were also immigrating to Canada. We kept up with our culture, our food, and religious faith as much as we could. I got my first job at the local shop where I was paid $3.65 an hour. My brother's first job was a paper route. My mum started taking food orders and baby-sitting to support the household income.

After completing Grade 13, I applied for university and attended the University of Toronto. I studied for a Bachelor of Commerce degree and graduated in 1987. Soon after, I landed my first professional job at Deloitte—fast forward 35 years later and I am still working at Deloitte, only now with much less hair on my head.

Progressing up the career ladder was challenging yet rewarding. I worked long hours during busy seasons, sleeping only a handful of hours a week. Similarly, my life apart from work was busy. I got married in June of 1989. We were a more established family at this stage, with each of us having our own jobs, our own set of friends, and our own responsibilities.

Unfortunately, my father passed away early on when we arrived in Canada. He couldn't see the fruits that came from the seeds that we planted together by immigrating here.

Advice to prospective new Canadians

There continued to be many challenges along the way, but recognizing where I came from, what we overcame as a family, allowed me to keep moving forward, maintaining hope for a brighter future.

HABIB MEGHJEE

is a partner at a global professional services firm. Habib has two grown children and continues to be an active member of his faith-based community.

Canada Offered Me More

David Jorjani

Iran

I was born in a small town in the northeast corner of Iran. When I was born, my mom wasn't working, and my dad would get paid every six months. To this day, I don't know how they made it work. My mom started working when I was two. Our family moved to another city when I was five, hoping that we would all have more opportunities. It took us years until we could afford to buy a piece of land to build our first home. I remember working with my brother and cousins and putting brick over brick to build our home. My dad had earned his civil engineering degree in the meantime, so we knew what we were doing. When I was thirteen, my mom enrolled at university for an undergraduate degree in accounting. She held her full- time job, finished her education, and raised three kids along the way.

I don't know how my parents pulled it off.

"I don't know how my parents pulled it off."

Fast forward to age 18, I was accepted to one of the best public universities in Iran and had to move away from family to Tehran, the capital. I had only been to Tehran once for two days and didn't know a single person in a busy city of 12 million people. It was scary and thrilling at the same time. As part of our public university education, our room and board were highly subsidized, and I learned to live on less than a dollar a day, which even for Iran was a tight budget. Having seen my mom work and study at the same time, I started working during my undergrad and made a little bit of money. I was very hopeful that I could make an impact in Iran and was excited to work and grow there. I was offered management of a promising project with one of the leading banks and could start my MBA at the University of Tehran directly after finishing my bachelor's degree. I had also made a lot of great friends and had learned to enjoy life. However, I soon realized the limitations of my future in Iran given the political and economic situation. I was also regularly reminded that I was a minority and there would not be a lot of room and support for growth. So, I decided to leave my country of birth.

I had never been to a western country. However, many of the graduates of our university had gone abroad for graduate school. I had the opportunity to talk to many people who were studying in the U.S., Europe, Australia, Asia, and Canada. There were four key factors in my decision.

- I wanted to belong. I didn't want to feel like a foreigner and be seen differently from everyone else around me. I did not want to have limits because of who I was or where I was born.

• I wanted to be able to grow as much as possible. Knowing that Canada, especially Toronto, welcomed immigrants and had a great economy allowed me to see my future there.

• I wanted peace of mind. Knowing that if I played my part right, I could become a Canadian in several years. This gave me the confidence I needed to decide.

• I wanted to live freely. Although I could go to more reputable universities and make more money in the U.S., it would have been a lot more difficult to travel or have my family visit me given the difficulties related to visa and immigration to the U.S., which has only worsened since then. I wanted to enjoy life in my best years and not just pursue material goals. Since arriving in Canada, I have been able to visit over twenty countries, visit my family twice and have my parents visit me twice.

Today, Toronto is home. I have a great career that allows me to do what I love and enjoy life. I also have the privilege of giving back. I have helped other immigrants find jobs in Toronto and I teach at the Department of Computer Science at the University of Toronto to help the next generation create the careers and lives they want.

My permanent residency process was mostly straightforward. As a graduate with a master's degree from the University of Toronto, I was able to apply through the Provincial Nominee Program of Ontario in March 2013 and became a permanent resident in 2014. In 2018, I became a Canadian citizen.

"The first year in Canada was certainly the most difficult."

Because of visa issues, I couldn't arrive in time to start my master's program and arrived well after the courses had started. I remember walking into my first classroom a few hours after my plane had landed. I was jetlagged, completely new, and oblivious to what was going on and certainly the odd one out. The professor spoke to me after the class and gave me a few more details about the course and on the assignment that was due soon.

The early days were the most difficult for me. My second cousin, who I hadn't even met before coming here, was the first person to help me in Canada. He picked me up from the airport and was kind enough to allow me to stay with them for the first week as I was searching for a place to rent. I remember walking around the city while he told me about Canadian Tire, Tim Hortons, and what to find where. Given my budget, I couldn't find a reasonable place to rent. After a week of searching, I was able to sublet the living room of a two-bedroom apartment close to campus from another student. One of my roommates was very kind and generous and taught me about life in Canada from an immigrant's perspective. I learned that hosting and welcoming new immigrants, even for a few days, may be an easy thing for locals to do but can have a lasting impact on immigrants. Knowing that, I became a mentor at the Centre for International Experience at the University of Toronto to help international students transition to Canada. I have been working with several non-profits to help other immigrants ever since.

Probably the biggest challenge in the first two years was the financial difficulties. Coming from a middle-class family in a small city in Iran and with limited income put a lot of stress on me. I had to watch where my money went very closely and didn't have the time, experience, or the legal right to work. After my first year, I got an amazing internship in Toronto, which would have solved my financial problems. But I couldn't do it because of the limitations of my visa.

I visited the U.S. many times in my first five years in Canada. I went to Seattle, Washington, New York, Boston, Chicago, San Francisco, and many other cities. I wanted to see if I had made the right decision to move to Toronto by seeing how those cities would compare. Comparing cities to live is mostly a personal and subjective matter and there are many ways to answer this question. For me, what mattered most was if I could truly feel like I belonged there by how the people would behave. In the U.S., I was often asked, "where are you originally from?" early in many conversations. The question, as simple as it seems, felt heavily loaded. Why did it matter where I came from?

The biggest highlight for me has been experiencing the diverse cultures and people from all over the world. For someone who didn't have the opportunity to travel to different places, having those cultures present in my city was a blessing. I enjoyed everything from the Taste of Danforth to Caribana to the Pride Parade. It opened my eyes to the world and things that I didn't even know existed.

Since moving here, I have certainly become more open-minded, accepting, and curious. I used to think that Iran had the best and richest culture and history in the world. I have seen many other ways of living life and have learned to look at them with a sense of wonder and ask questions to learn. I have come to realize that every culture and every person has a unique perspective and an interesting story. I have found many similarities under the surface that connect our cultures.

It takes courage to leave everything behind for a completely new and uncertain world. Immigration usually has a difficult start with a desirable end but staying can be challenging.

Thankfully, there is more support in Canada than anywhere else for someone to come and start from scratch, for which I am grateful. Immigration is an investment in the future with an expensive initial payment. More often than not, it pays off. Looking at the larger, more long-term picture, it costs more to stay stagnant where we are than to move to a new place with more opportunities.

Today, I am proud to say that I am Canadian.

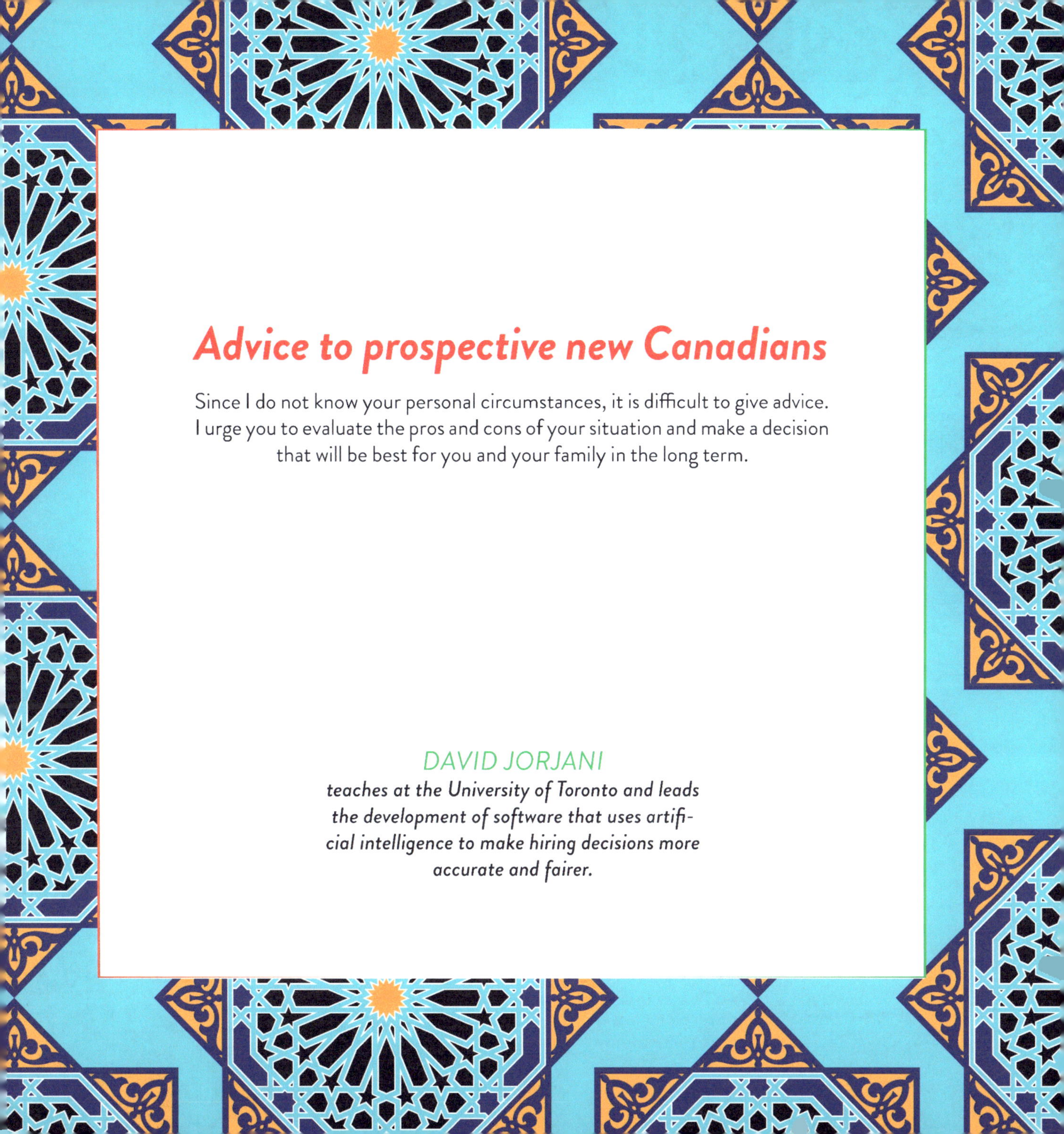

Advice to prospective new Canadians

Since I do not know your personal circumstances, it is difficult to give advice. I urge you to evaluate the pros and cons of your situation and make a decision that will be best for you and your family in the long term.

DAVID JORJANI

teaches at the University of Toronto and leads the development of software that uses artificial intelligence to make hiring decisions more accurate and fairer.

It Was Cold...But, in the End Very Warm

Arslan Mahmood

Pakistan

I was born in Rawalpindi, and grew up in Islamabad, Pakistan. I have a younger sister and a brother. Both of my parents were moderately educated. My father worked in a bank all his life. My mother was a stay-at-home mom and took care of all our needs growing up. From a very young age, I was ambitious and independent. I worked part-time jobs to partially pay for my university and to support myself. When I finished my university, I was offered an entry level position at a large air-conditioning manufacturing company in Islamabad. It was an exciting yet challenging job for a recent graduate. I was enjoying the challenge and progressing successfully.

After a few years of working at the company, I started exploring options for studying abroad. When I spoke with my family, my father's first reaction was that he could not support my studies abroad with his income. I started saving money to realise my dreams of studying abroad. All in all, life was good and worry free.

It all changed with the sudden passing of my father. With the loss, a huge responsibility fell on my shoulders; the responsibility of taking care of all aspects of running the house, finances, and much more. This was all new and unexpected, but my family was there to support me. My dream of leaving was put aside for some time. After a year, I brought back the idea of studying abroad to my mother. By this time, I had some savings to support myself in my travels. My mother's response was positive, and, at the time, she was fully occupied with the wedding planning of my younger sister. I started exploring again.

"The first day in a new country is always memorable."

Canada's reputation as a country to study for foreign students was increasing in the mid-90s. Top contenders for this type of education were the United Kingdom, United States of America, and Australia. For me, Canada became a choice because of the cost of studying and living, and the possibility of immigrating in the future. The decision to choose Canada was made easier when my cousin immigrated to Canada with his family around the same time I received an offer of admission from a college in Toronto, Canada. I connected with my cousin to check the college and its reputation. Once I heard that all was good, I confirmed my admissions, and paid the tuition fee. I applied and received a Canadian visa. The week after my sister's wedding, I was on the plane to Canada!

My stay in Canada was as an international student. As such, I was eligible to obtain an open work permit after completing my studies. When I graduated, I received an open work permit for a year. My plan was to apply for permanent residency (PR) within six months of the open work permit. I did my research and started gathering supporting documents. I applied and waited for the favorable outcome. The whole PR process from the application to the interview took over a year.

Finally, I received a letter from Canadian Immigration. My heart started to beat at a high pace. I opened the letter and the first word that caught my attention was "denied". Yes, my application for permanent residency was denied due to the lack of evidence of my work experience related to the category under which I applied. I will never forget the day, I felt numb for a while. I had to read the letter few times to fully comprehend and accept the fact that my application was denied, and that I must leave Canada immediately.

My first thought was to consult with my friends and family, and to retain an immigration lawyer. After a few consultations with the lawyer, I decided to apply for PR again. I also needed to extend my visitor visa for another six months to remain in Canada. We made some changes in the new PR application and submitted it. This time, the waiting was difficult because I was now staying in Canada as a visitor, unable to work or study.

After a year of waiting, I finally received a letter from Canadian Immigration to appear for an interview in Detroit, U.S.A. I prepared for the interview with the immigration lawyer. This time, I felt the interview went much better. There were not as many questions asked as before. After the interview, the immigration office requested my passport and asked if I would like to get the PR documents in few hours. When I heard that my application was approved, I was so relieved. I returned to the immigration office and received my PR papers and entered Canada via the Detroit-Windsor border one more time, this time as a permanent resident of Canada.

I must say, the information and process of applying for the permanent residency was clearly laid out in the Canadian Immigration website. Anyone can apply without help from an immigration lawyer. In my case, I learned that my interpretation of each work category differed from that of the immigration officer. My advice to potential applicants would be that if you have any doubts about your application, consult a lawyer. These professionals handle immigration related cases regularly and could make a difference in your application.

The first day in a new country is always memorable. For me, it certainly was. I arrived in Canada on the last day of December. When I stepped out of the airport, I was welcomed by a December cold breeze. At first, it was refreshing, but in few minutes, my body was in shock. I was fortunate that my cousin came to the airport and took me to his place in a taxi. Even with a little exposure to the wind, I must say, I felt very cold.

After few hours of my arrival, my cousin's family and I decided to venture out to celebrate New Year's Eve. We went to Nathan Phillips

Square, an open square in front of Toronto's City Hall. We used a subway train (underground train) to get to our destination. Everything was new to me. I thought it was a very civil way of travelling, compared to my home country. I noticed that the train passengers minded their own business. The ride was quiet and comfortable. I enjoyed my first subway train experience thoroughly.

At Nathan Phillips Square, a large crowd covered in layers of clothing, were enjoying the festivities. I was taking it all in, including my very first experience of being outside under the clear sky on a very cold night. It didn't take long for my feet to start to freeze. After moving and jumping to keep the blood flowing, the cold temperature became unbearable. To take a break, we all went to a nearby coffee shop, Tim Hortons. My cousin told me that it was a famous Canadian coffee chain. I was not a coffee drinker but tried a "double-double" coffee. I was told that double-double means two spoons of sugar and two spoons of cream in a coffee. It certainly felt good and warmed the body.

I had good intentions to stay till midnight and see the countdown to welcome the New Year. However, I was only able to survive a few hours in the frigid weather. We returned home early. I discovered very quickly that I needed to buy proper winter boots and a coat for the Canadian winter. The clothes that I bought from Pakistan were not made for the Canadian climate. One piece of advice for readers; if you are planning to settle in Canada, please buy your winter clothing in Canada. It may be expensive, but certainly worth the investment.

The first few days in Canada were exciting and memorable. Everything was new and exhilarating, and my cousins were taking care of me and showing me around. It ended very quickly when my cousins went back to their routine, and I began my studies.

My journey from this point was a hard one. I had my cousins, but I had to take care of myself. I searched for a rental place close to my college and moved. Making new friends, getting settled in a new rental place, finding the rhythm of going to school, and looking for a part-time job was challenging. The most urgent and difficult part in all of this was finding a part-time job. The savings I had brought with me were diminishing fast, and I did not have the option of asking my mother to send me money because she had no source of income back in Pakistan. Looking for part-time work in Canada was also a new experience because I had never worked here before. I used the career centre at my college to help me update my resume, guide me as to where to look for jobs, and how I should appear for an interview. While I was a student in Canada, I had limitations and could only work on-campus where I was studying. There were many international students in a similar situation, therefore job prospects on campus were limited and competition was high. With persistence and a positive attitude, I was able to secure my first part-time job. This helped me to stay focused on my studies and I was able to complete them successfully.

Over time, I was able to make new friends, most of them were students at my college. I was spending my time either in classes, working, or with my friends. I felt having friends was very important as it provided me with a support network to discuss any challenges and to share successes. It was a great comfort knowing that I could speak to someone when I needed.

Living alone with roommates was also new for me. I had never experienced this before. I was lucky that in a short time these roommates became my close friends. But getting into the routine of cleaning the apartment, doing laundry, making meals, and buying groceries was still difficult. Income from work was just enough to buy groceries and to pay rent. I couldn't believe how fast a month went by when you were paying rent. This was the reality and there was no escape.

The lessons that I learned from these experiences were to stay positive, to be persistent, and to stay flexible to overcome challenges.

Slowly and steadily, I adjusted to life in Canada. My journey thus far had not been easy, but I started feeling comfortable and became more confident that I could do many things myself. In the early days I was very hesitant to use the city transit system alone, or order food. Now, I was helping others with similar tasks.

"It took about six months to really get comfortable in Canada."

I settled into a routine of studying, working, and living alone. I had a group of friends that I was spending time with on weekends. We went to many festivals and had many picnics in and around Toronto. One of our friends had a car. We all contributed money to go even further out of Toronto to explore parks and lakes on summer weekends. Life was becoming normal and getting homesick was no longer top of mind. Steady income was coming from my part-time job, which allowed me to do these activities with my friends. Studies were going smoothly. The balance of work, study, and pleasure was getting better.

As I mentioned earlier, the first six months were more challenging, but with time life felt more normal. Finishing my studies successfully and on time was very important to me. It was necessary to apply for permanent residency (PR) and employment in Canada. I was lucky that when I started applying for full-time jobs, I was somewhat familiar with the Canadian job market as I had worked part time throughout my studies. I attended job fairs at my college and in the community where I was living. I consulted with my professors, career coordinators, and friends on how to apply for jobs. I sent my resume through online postings to a network of college professors and career coordinators.

After sending many resumes, I was successful on getting a few interview calls. These turned into an offer right after completing my studies. I was relieved yet anxious to start my new career in Canada. My goal was to obtain full-time employment and to apply for permanent residency right after completing my studies. Even though I thought the PR process would be easy, it became a challenge when my first application was rejected. Luckily, the second attempt was successful.

From the time I arrived in Canada, every experience, had an impact on my life, shaping who I am today. I came to Canada with strong values and beliefs. Experience and being open-minded here certainly reinforced and validated these. Living in Toronto was amazing, but when I travelled outside the city within the province of Ontario, I really began to appreciate the size of this country. I was lucky to travel across the province with my work colleagues, and it was the best Canadian experience I had had at that point.

During my work trips, I visited high schools across the province. I met students and families from the Indigenous peoples of Canada to

"I really began to appreciate the size of this country."

settlers of many generations. Some of these high schools were in very small communities. The simplicity and politeness I encountered throughout my trips was incredible. I experienced first-hand Canadian passion for the sport of ice-hockey. I attended some hockey games in small communities where young kids, parents, uncles and aunts, grandparents, and neighbors all gathered to watch and cheer for their young players. I felt a strong sense of community. I loved dining in many small family-owned restaurants during these trips. Hospitality was marvelous and no matter how far I was from my city, I was treated like I was at home.

My travels also took me to communities in Ontario that were once thriving and then became ghost towns. Factories were closing, and people were leaving to find jobs in other places. I could imagine how challenging it would be to attract families back if there were no jobs. All of this really impacted the way I saw Canada. I appreciated the size of the province with its beautiful countryside with abundance of water (lakes). It is a place to discover. The quote on the Ontario license plate, Yours to Discover relates to my experience. I do now appreciate the vastness of this place.

Life in Canada has its own charm. In the

beginning, it was hard, and I needed some time to adjust. But with time, it got better. For me, life here is peaceful. I feel safe and accepted. It is clean and offers all the amenities like roads, transits, shopping malls, libraries, schools, hospitals, community centers, etc. Canada is an open and welcoming place for all and appreciates and celebrates diversity. Some may take all this for granted and may not even think and appreciate what we have, but when we travel outside of Canada, we are reminded how privileged and lucky we are.

I came to Canada from a very homogenous society, where most of us have the same religion and language. Diversity existed in cultures in different parts of the country, but these were not always open and inclusive. Living and working in Toronto has allowed me to understand and respect many cultures. I would say my perspective on culture and diversity has changed. I have learned to respect others, which means I try to learn and understand before making any judgments.

"Canada is a country that embraces new immigrants."

I have observed Canada's commitment to attracting new immigrants at every level of the government, from federal to provincial to municipal. Living in such a diverse place may also bring some challenges with respect to shared values and beliefs. I learned that when I am open and accepting, I do not feel threatened; I feel that my own beliefs are strengthened. Also, adjusting to life in Canada at a young age as a college student was easier and faster than if I would have come here at a later stage of my life. Everyone's situation may be unique, but those who are planning to make Canada their home must do some research. If possible, visit Canada before moving permanently, and speak with your friends and family who are already living here.

There are many crises around the world from natural disasters to civil unrest. Canada is at the forefront when it comes to offering humanitarian support. We continue to open our doors to accommodate refugees for temporary or permanent settlement when necessary. On the other hand, after traveling through northern Ontario, and listening to news regularly, I must say that Canada has its own humanitarian crises. There is a constant reduction in funding for healthcare, and education. Big cities like Toronto are facing affordable housing issues. Smaller communities in the north are facing challenges of their own. It is hard to believe that some communities in the far north don't have clean drinking water.

It is important for us to help other countries, but it is also important to pay attention and support our own citizens first.

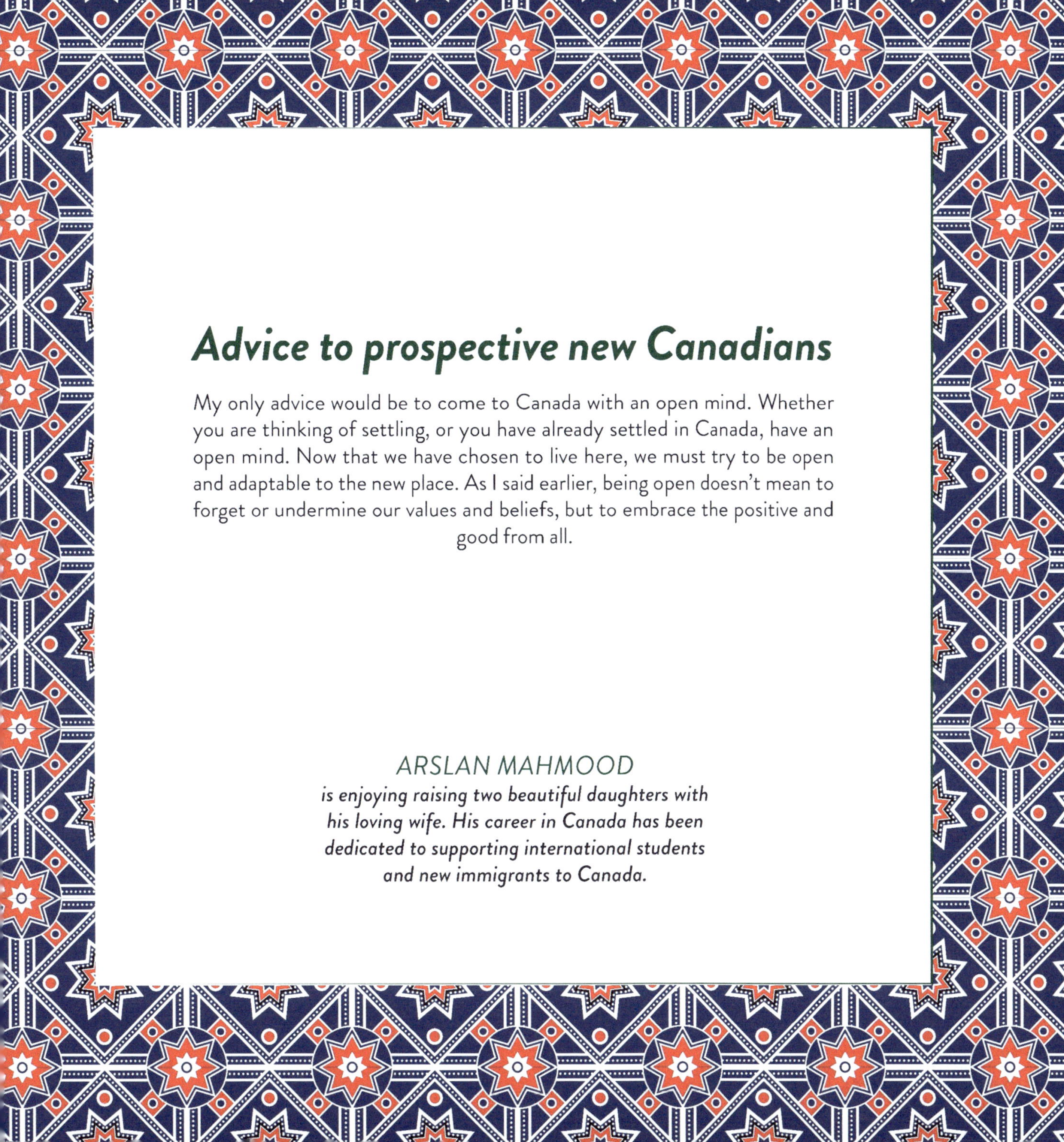

Advice to prospective new Canadians

My only advice would be to come to Canada with an open mind. Whether you are thinking of settling, or you have already settled in Canada, have an open mind. Now that we have chosen to live here, we must try to be open and adaptable to the new place. As I said earlier, being open doesn't mean to forget or undermine our values and beliefs, but to embrace the positive and good from all.

ARSLAN MAHMOOD

is enjoying raising two beautiful daughters with his loving wife. His career in Canada has been dedicated to supporting international students and new immigrants to Canada.

From Rags to Riches to Canada

Juan Lopez

Nicaragua

I had a good life in Nicaragua. My father had a business, and I obtained a business degree which allowed me to manage it. We were not rich people, but we were comfortable. I was married with two young boys. We lived in our own home and had staff who took care of us.

It was politically unstable in my country and there was a civil war. When the guerillas took power, my father and brother-in-law, both of whom had attachments to the government, had to leave the country. After my father left, I had many problems because I had the same name as my father. The guerillas confused me with my father and once I was put in jail for seven days. Every single night they would come to my cell and tell me that they would take me out to the field to kill me if I did not confess that I was against the guerillas. My secretary, who fought with the guerillas against the government, knew me well and she knew I had nothing to do with the previous government. She went to speak with one of the guerilla commandants to advocate for my life. Thankfully, I was released. But even after I was released, I received calls threatening harm to myself and my family if I did not give money. I decided to leave the country. I had to escape, leaving all my family money.

I left my country for the United States. I asked for political asylum because I was incarcerated, harassed, and had two young sons. The guerilla government could have taken my sons at any time to serve in the army (child soldiers). My petition for asylum was denied in the U.S. I had permission to work but not permanent status. At this time, a friend of mine told me that the Canadian Consulate in Atlanta, Georgia, was coming to Miami, Florida once a month to interview people who wanted to immigrate to Canada. I went to the interview with the help of a translator as I did not speak English.

"I believe that Canada was looking for people that would be an asset to the country."

The consul asked me about my life. I told him that there was a 180-degree change. I went from working an air-conditioned office to digging holes in the streets of Miami in 90-degree heat. That was in the daytime. At night, I was cleaning toilets in office buildings.

I believe that day was my lucky day. The officer asked me when I wanted to immigrate to Canada. I told him I wanted to leave yesterday. He said to wait a week and he would send me a letter that would allow me to go to Canada and that as soon as I arrived in the country, I would become a landed immigrant. Two weeks later I packed my family into a car and drove to Canada. We arrived December 10, 1983. We were not prepared for the winter. At the border, we were sent to a hotel in downtown Toronto, Ontario to stay until we could find a place to live. We went to the Salvation Army to buy winter coats and boots.

I believe that Canada was looking for people that would be an asset to the country, people who would be able to do any job to support his or her family. Another person who went for an interview was a doctor back home but was not accepted as he was much more particular about the types of jobs he would do in Canada.

Before I left my country and moved to the U.S., I experienced discrimination as a non-white person. This happened less when I came to Canada.

I came to Canada in the winter of 1983. It was cold. I was not used to this kind of weather. The only ice I knew before was the one I had in my drink. Learning to walk on ice was a challenge.

My sons were enrolled in school. They enjoyed learning a new language. They were well-accepted and easily integrated into society. My then-wife and I enrolled in English classes and looked for work.

Someone in the hotel told us that there were Nicaraguan people living in Scarborough. We moved there so we could be close to people who shared our customs, culture, and language.

For the first time in many years, I went to sleep without the fear of somebody coming to my house to kill me and my family. New starts are never easy, but if you work hard and persevere you will be successful. I remember when I was looking for a job, the first question employers asked was if I had "Canadian Experience". How can you get Canadian experience if you have never lived or worked in the country? Another highlight was voting for the first time in Canada. In my country, our votes did not count.

The biggest challenge was the language. I did not understand anyone and because of that, people thought I was inferior. I was treated as a second-class citizen. I got a job working on an assembly line at one of the biggest automakers in Canada. The job was hard but dealing with the people around me was harder. I was not welcomed at all. People told me that because of all the immigrants coming to Canada, their children would not have a job in the future.

"I noticed that the people who discriminated most against me had much less education than I did."

I had a university degree, while many of them had not even finished high school.

Judy was the immigration representative who took my case. I reported to her every month. The immigration program allowed you and your family to go to school and learn English and the government supported you and your family for one year. From the beginning, I expressed my desire to work... the sooner the better. I started to look for any job, but again I had no Canadian experience. Three months into the program, Judy told me that General Motors (GM) was hiring, and she knew the right person to talk to. Thanks to Judy, I got the job. It was my only real job in Canada until I retired five years ago. I worked on the line and in management. I will be grateful to Judy all my life.

I always say to friends and family that Canada is my country. I am pleased and proud to live in Canada knowing that my children are growing in a peaceful environment where we have health coverage, and a government that cares about the environment and respects the law. Carrying a Canadian passport is a privilege and honour for me. I love Canada. I married a Canadian woman and had two sons with her.

I have learned to keep my chin up. Discrimination is not the same today as it was in the 1980s, but it still exists. In many ways, things have changed in the last 20 years for the better.

Advice to prospective new Canadians

I would tell prospective immigrants that it is important to integrate into Canadian society while maintaining your own customs. Be flexible and open to change. Do not take Canada for granted. Work hard, respect the law, and learn English and you will have a great life in Canada.
The world should look at Canada as an example of compassion, respect, and inclusion.

JUAN LOPEZ
is retired and lives in Ontario with his wife, four sons and daughter-in-law. He loves being an abuelo to his beautiful granddaughter.

Canada Was Part of My Destiny

Rania Mohy El Din Nafea

Egypt

I have always been on the move. I was born in Cairo and raised in Dubai, UAE. When the time came for university, I got accepted in one of the most prestigious universities in Egypt—The American University in Cairo (AUC). The first 'American University' in the region, offering quality, liberal thinking education.

After graduation, I chose to join HSBC bank and was accepted into their 'executive training program'. An added bonus was meeting my husband while in the training program. As you can see, it was a good choice! In 2002, I received an offer from the British American Tobacco Company. They offered an insight to both the finance and marketing side of private companies, a whole new world that I was interested in exploring.

At the end of 2003, my husband received an offer in Abu Dhabi. Although that meant leaving my job and relocating, I was happy at the thought of returning home to the UAE again, where I had spent the best years of my life. The transition was smooth, and although I got a job teaching, I had time on my hands. I decided to use my time studying for a PhD program. It was at this time that the idea of immigrating to Canada started to shine like a star.

Middle Eastern women, in general, are notorious for nagging their husbands. I was no different. It's part of our DNA! I nagged my husband to apply for immigration to Canada

"I could not understand the school policy or the 'Canadian way' of dealing with things."

and we started the application with myself as the primary applicant. Although the paperwork was lengthy and detailed, we managed to submit our application in 2005. Many years would pass before we received any news about our immigration application and in In August 2009 we landed in Canada!

At the time my kids were only three and two respectively. As a family, we decided to explore our new home. We started off by staying in a cozy hotel in Mississauga for two weeks, during which time we would explore options of where to stay. A good education for our children was a priority as well as managing a financial budget to create stability. During this time, we had a million thoughts passing through our heads; was a life in Canada worth it, especially if my husband had to support us? Would I find a teaching job easily? How do we both overcome the 'Canadian Experience' dilemma? As a result of these questions, we decided to consider this trip as a family vacation with no strings attached to settle in Canada.

Everything changed for us in 2011. A revolution erupted in Egypt and the 'Arab Spring' swept across North Africa and signs of political instability started to manifest. My husband and I had mixed feelings. We were anxious about the future of Egypt... Could we go back one day? How long would it take for this uncertainty to calm down. Was it our destiny to settle in Canada? In 2012, we made the decision to settle down permanently in Canada.

North York became our new home in August 12, 2012 and will remain so for the next nine years. The first few weeks were spent applying for health cards and drivers' licenses. My husband stayed with us until he had to leave for his job in Saudi Arabia in September.

I will never forget the day he left. It was heart wrenching. Both kids were crying as they could not fathom why their father had to leave. I was in tears and could not imagine living and being responsible for two kids without any support from family or friends. My husband burst into tears as he rode away to the airport. It was a miserable day in my life. At that point, I hated Canada!

The first three years were a living hell. My solace was my best friend from university (SY). I had known SY since my early university years and we also knew each other's families back home. She was my family. I spent the weekends at her home in Oakville. Yes, it was a long drive, but she was the only adult I could talk to at the time. She was my rock. My condo neighbour also did her best introducing me to the Egyptian community in North York and driving me around to Halal stores to pick up my groceries. Yet, I still hated Canada—It didn't feel like home.

I tried to find work during my first year in Toronto, but it seemed harder than Tom Cruise's 'Mission impossible'. Some obstacles were certificate equivalencies and the 'Canadian experience'. Since many employers would often say to me 'Well, you seem qualified, but how do I really know what your qualifications mean?' To overcome that, I sent all my certificates for the necessary equivalencies. I also made the brave decision at the end of my first year—to go back to school. I enrolled in the College Teacher's Training Program (CTTP) at George Brown College. This programme helps qualified professionals, with a minimum of a master's degree, to join the College teaching community. In essence it serves as a bridging program. I wish I had known about this and the equivalencies prior to my arrival in Canada.

I worked very hard in the programme in order to make a good impression and my efforts paid off when one of my professors recommended me for a job at George Brown College in their Continuing Education program and I juggled my studies and nighttime teaching. This challenging schedule was difficult for my young children.

While my daughter was in school, she encountered bullying, and this was something new for me to manage. I could not understand the school policy or the 'Canadian way' of dealing with things. I honestly couldn't wrap my head around how kids were asked to be civil to bullies and not respond. Anyhow, I convinced my daughter about the importance of the policy and gave her rules about managing conflict, but I don't think any of it resonated!

In 2014, I flew to the Netherlands to defend my DBA thesis. I was excited to learn that I would finally get the opportunity to achieve the highest academic degree in my field. In my culture, being a doctor is a very prestigious achievement. I felt a sense of pride and my self-esteem went through the roof. I was glad that my sister was by my side for this significant milestone.

One of the key lessons I learned during the past 9 years was that you can never really plan ahead! My husband left his work in Saudi Arabia, and this opened a whole new door of debate and uncertainty. Will he decide to reside in Canada or go back home to Egypt?

What's the right decision? Well guess what... there' is no right decision. We are responsible for our choices and their consequences.

My husband decided to go back to Egypt to take care of his mother and resume his career. The only challenge was that the Egyptian income would not allow him to support us the way he did earlier on, and my part time job wouldn't be enough to cover the difference. But I guess God works in mysterious ways. In May 2015, a recruiter contacted me about a full-time professor position at Seneca College. What followed were a series of interviews and I was officially part of the Seneca faculty.

I was disappointed with my husband's decision at the time, and part of me still is. It was a turning point in our lives. I mentally understood his reasons for this decision, especially with him being the older and more reliable sibling. Yet, there is a part of me that questions this decision until today. What if he had chosen to come to Canada? We would have been reunited as a family... would the kids have been raised in a different way with him being around? Would we have been more financially stable and secure with two Canadian incomes? Many questions came to mind then and still do from time to time. I felt like the less significant part of this equation. I had hopes that his parents would ask him to reconsider his decisions and advise him on the importance of his presence in Canada with the kids. Middle Eastern parents tend to manifest selfish traits and protect their children like bears. Don't get me wrong, they want what's best for their kids, but *only* their kids. Daughters-in-law are usually an unwanted extension.

In 2016, a series of unfortunate events interrupted my life. I was diagnosed with a disease in its early stages, and I was concerned about the treatment and my kids. I knew that I had to fight. I did not shed a tear until weeks later when it all hit me, and I felt overwhelmed. I was a whirlpool of emotions, and the dominant feeling was that of frustration and anger. I was furious with my husband for not choosing to come to Canada.

Two months later, after my recovery, I was involved in a huge car accident on the 401 highways. The accident resulted in whiplash and severe back pain. This was a difficult time for me—emotionally, physical, and mentally. I thank God for the community of friends around me that stood by my side. AH, MS, MR, NZ and MF—you ladies are the rock! Life continued. I was a mom and a dad, working full-time, being a driver, a cook, a nanny, and a therapist as the kids grew older.

Despite a number of challenges, I continued to focus on self-development and this allowed me to grow. My work at Seneca afforded me the opportunity to travel and I was invited to use my skills for a teaching opportunity in New Delhi, India.

The highlight of the year came in November 2018, when we took our citizenship oath. We were now finally Canadians! There was a sense of pride and accomplishment for sure. Yet, it came with another question—now what? Go back home? Stay here? What about my marriage? There was a lot to think of especially with my daughter going into high school in 2019. I think we were both scared of taking a decision. We weren't sure what to do since we were now taking a decision that would impact the kids too.

I joined TRIEC (Toronto Region Immigrant Employment Council) as a mentor for new immigrants who need guidance in the business and teaching field. Almost everyone I mentored was frustrated with the challenges faced by immigrants. Much more work is required to ensure that immigrants are given opportunities in senior level roles and that their skills and experiences are recognized.

The experience has been tough and overwhelming to say the least. If you read my story, you might get the impression that I am not grateful to be in Canada. On the contrary, I am grateful and blessed for the opportunity to be here and live in a multicultural community. I believe that Canada was part of my destiny. Yes, there are frustrations and struggles, but there has also been a myriad of opportunities for personal success and as my kids grow older, I am proud of how they've flourished. I am proud of how my daughter has overcome her struggles at school and has transformed into a smart and ambitious social butterfly and how my son is becoming the man I've always wanted him to be. Canada has made them unique and different… Yet, if you're immigrating as a single mom, the road is bumpy ahead and you have to be ready to 'accept the challenge'!

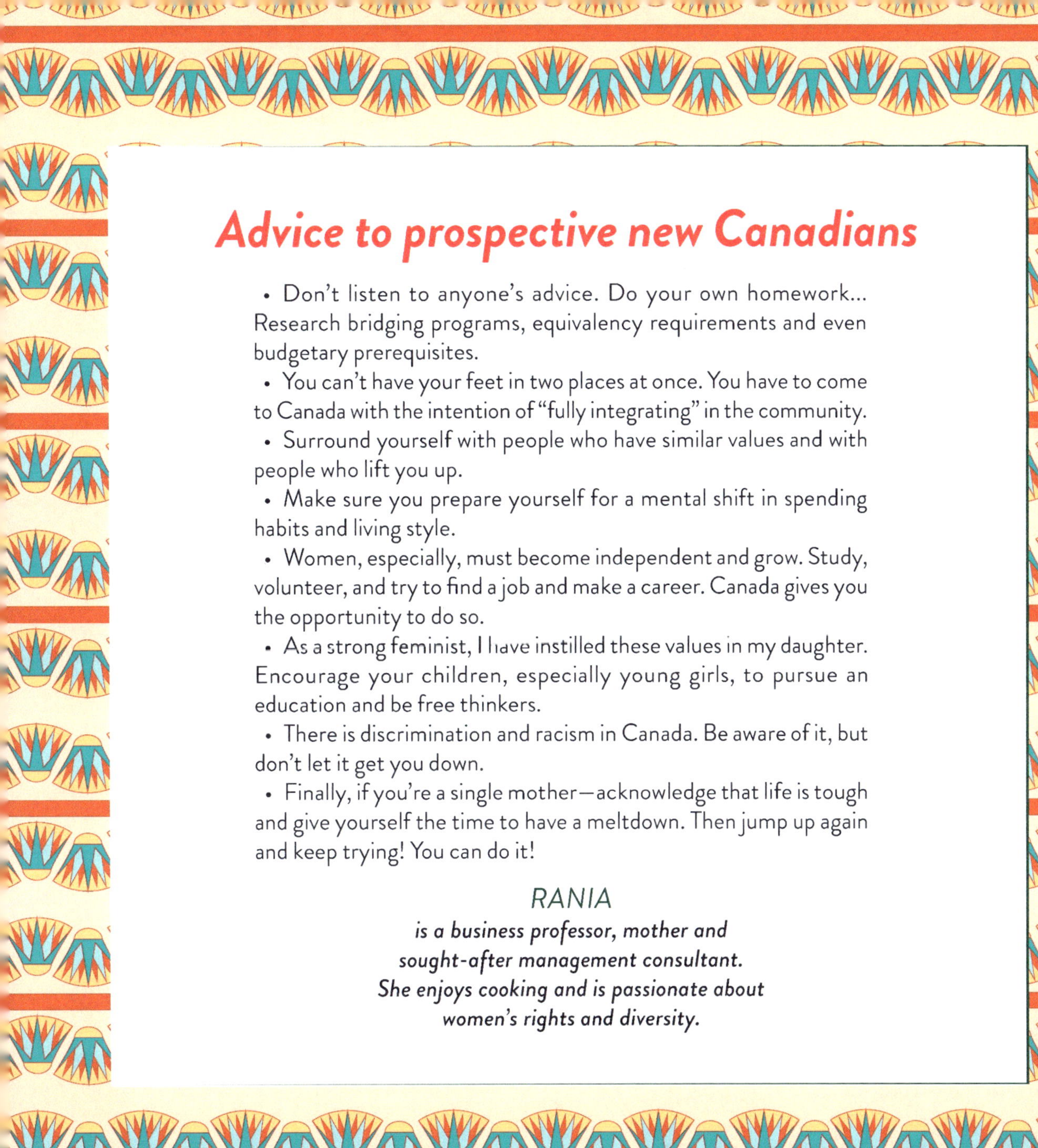

Advice to prospective new Canadians

- Don't listen to anyone's advice. Do your own homework... Research bridging programs, equivalency requirements and even budgetary prerequisites.
- You can't have your feet in two places at once. You have to come to Canada with the intention of "fully integrating" in the community.
- Surround yourself with people who have similar values and with people who lift you up.
- Make sure you prepare yourself for a mental shift in spending habits and living style.
- Women, especially, must become independent and grow. Study, volunteer, and try to find a job and make a career. Canada gives you the opportunity to do so.
- As a strong feminist, I have instilled these values in my daughter. Encourage your children, especially young girls, to pursue an education and be free thinkers.
- There is discrimination and racism in Canada. Be aware of it, but don't let it get you down.
- Finally, if you're a single mother—acknowledge that life is tough and give yourself the time to have a meltdown. Then jump up again and keep trying! You can do it!

RANIA

is a business professor, mother and sought-after management consultant. She enjoys cooking and is passionate about women's rights and diversity.

Just Lovely

Zelo Soyalp

Turkey

> **"My permanent resident application process was long and overdrawn. "**

I was a young professional who just graduated from university in Istanbul. I took a good job in a private consulting firm. I loved Istanbul but life wasn't easy there with millions of people, frustrating commutes, and long hours. I knew that I wanted to pursue graduate studies abroad.

Coming to Canada was a combination of choice, coincidence, and luck. I wanted to pursue a master's degree abroad. However, I did not have the funds to do so. Tuition fees for international students were too high. I needed a scholarship and ability to work during my studies. I did some research and it seemed that amongst the English-speaking countries, only the U.S. and Canada offered scholarships. I applied to several schools to increase my chances. I was admitted to three of them but only two offered scholarships and a job as a graduate teaching assistant. It was a choice between Ohio State University in the U.S. and Queen's University in Kingston, Ontario. I knew nothing about Ohio or Kingston; I did not have a way of choosing between the two. I asked an economics professor I knew at the time. He was an eccentric person, very smart, and well-travelled in North America. He said," Kingston has good bars!" So, I chose Queen's University and arrived in Kingston six months later.

My permanent resident application process was long and overdrawn. I initially arrived as a master's student on a student visa. At the time there was no program for students to transition to permanent residents. (There was no "Canadian Experience" class.) I applied for a work permit afterwards. My work permit was denied on account of the date on my diploma being one week later than the date on the job offer. I was trying to be proactive by applying for a job before graduation, however, this worked against me. I applied again with the same job and same diploma (asked the employer to change the job offer date by two weeks) and got the work permit. I applied for permanent residence as a skilled worker in the meantime. My application was denied for not having enough points. I consulted an expert and they told me that a mistake had been made and I should appeal the decision. At the same time, the point system changed. (They lowered the points.) I now met the point system without a doubt. I debated between appealing the former decision or applying again under the new system. I was living with my boyfriend at the time and learned that living with a partner was considered a common-law marriage. I preferred to apply independently but my boyfriend heard that applying under the spousal system was faster. He insisted we finish this long process of immigration and just apply under spousal. So, we did; I got permanent residency shortly after. (We are still married.) My years spent as a student with a work permit did not count towards my time in Canada during the citizenship process. I was eligible to apply a few years after. I got my citizenship 10 years after my arrival in Canada.

I was a master's student during my first 12 months. It was lovely. I made Canadian friends at school. Canadians are lovely people. On my first day I stayed with the international student advisor at the school. She put yogurt on her fruit salad. I never saw that before. To this day this is still what I eat for breakfast. She offered me her couch the night I arrived. Some other people on the street (walking their dogs) told me not to wait for the bus as there was no bus at 9p.m. in Kingston. Canadians are great.

The highlight during my first five years was receiving my permanent residence status after a few years of waiting. The day I found my first job I felt like my dreams had come true. Uncertainty was a big challenge. Not knowing if I would stay or go, find a job, or stay with my boyfriend was hard to deal with.

My husband made the biggest impact on me. He was my friend during grad school. (There was a bus strike affecting students coming from the residence. He drove us to the grocery store. Such a nice guy!) I learned so much from him about multicultural Canada. Then he became my boyfriend and my biggest supporter during the immigration process. I have yet to meet someone as special. We married and had a beautiful daughter a few years ago.

"I adopted multiculturalism."

My home country doesn't encourage diversity, but I adopted cultural pluralism as an attitude. I love Canadians in all their different colors. I became more open-minded and less judgmental about people. I embraced a middle-class lifestyle where one can clean your own house and not worry about impressing guests and hosting. I became more easy-going.

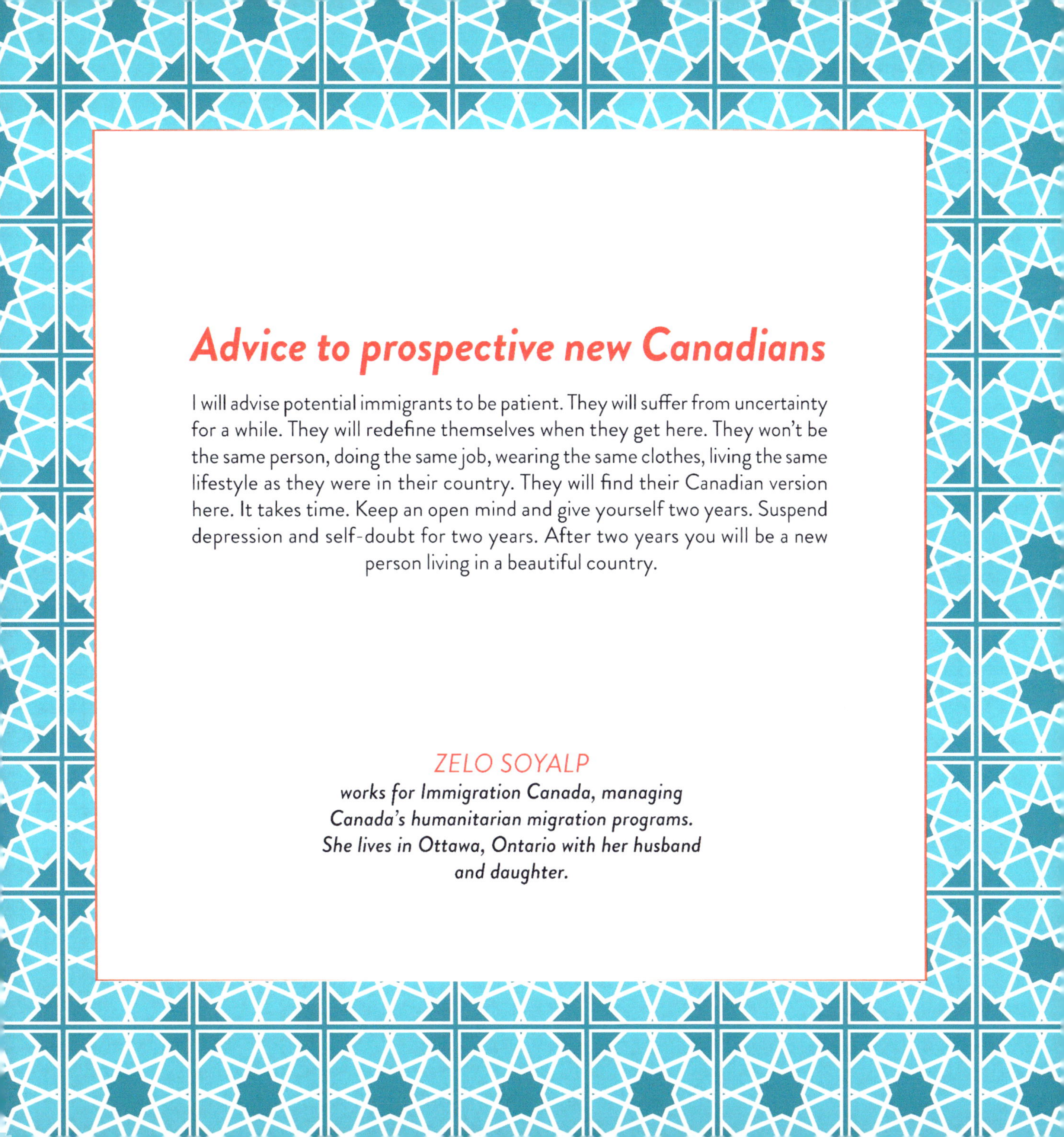

Advice to prospective new Canadians

I will advise potential immigrants to be patient. They will suffer from uncertainty for a while. They will redefine themselves when they get here. They won't be the same person, doing the same job, wearing the same clothes, living the same lifestyle as they were in their country. They will find their Canadian version here. It takes time. Keep an open mind and give yourself two years. Suspend depression and self-doubt for two years. After two years you will be a new person living in a beautiful country.

ZELO SOYALP

works for Immigration Canada, managing Canada's humanitarian migration programs. She lives in Ottawa, Ontario with her husband and daughter.

This Roller Coaster Ride Was Definitely Worth It

Sina Dejnabadi

Iran

I was 31 when I immigrated to Canada. In the years prior to immigration, I worked in an international company in Tehran that represented globally renowned names such as Bosch and General Electric (GE) in Iran. I started working at 18, a few months after finishing high school. I initially entered the company in 1996. In 14 years, I my responsibilities went from those of a clerk who entered data for the hydropower plant equipment, to becoming the oil and gas director with supervision of U.S.$80 millions of sales to refineries, petrochemicals, oil and gas pipelines, and oil tank terminals. At the age 30 I was managing a team of 12 in sales, marketing, and engineering.

I can describe my life in the years preceding immigration in just one word: Luxurious. As a twenty-something kid, I was working as a high-ranking executive in an international company. I had my spacious office in one of the most prestigious office buildings in Tehran. I had my own driver and was earning over $150,000 a year in Iran (The minimum wage was $7,500 a year by that time). I was travelling business class abroad seven or eight times each year and living in a good neighborhood in the city.

I graduated from university in industrial engineering; however, my passion was in sales and marketing with a focus on oil and gas equipment for national and international projects.

During the 13 years I worked for that

"Canada, its values, and culture, encouraged me to think about community rather than focusing on myself."

company, I tried multiple times to quit my job and launch my own business without success. My first attempt was in 1998 when I was only 20 years old. I started a small business as the representative of a U.K. company but as a kid with little money in hand, my boss convinced me to come back for triple the income. The second time it happened, I was 24, and I started a new company with my father. We had financial ups and downs and my boss came to my father again and asked him to push me back to my job with an even higher income. I was doing my mandatory military service, and I was about to be married so I thought the offer was amazing as I needed the steady income, so I succumbed and went back.

I finished my almost two years of mandatory services in 2004. As part of my job, I was travelling to Europe quite frequently. I was very happy about all these trips and the experiences of meeting high-industrial executives and their companies. I had to get visa every time I wanted to travel. The process of applying for visa in Iran was very time consuming and exhausting. I also had to stand in a line and answer questions about the reason for my trip every single time. My boss, who was a carrying a British passport, was passing through quickly with no questions.

As a young person, I wanted to travel freely, and I didn't like these delays and long procedures.

One day in 2005, at the house of a friend I noticed a magazine on a coffee table opened to an article about life in Toronto. I remember saying to my wife and friends, "Guys, don't you think we could travel more freely and respectfully? We would have a better quality of life in Canada. Look at the pictures of our next home, it's amazing! I think I may immigrate to Canada".

Right after the gathering with our friends, my wife and I decided to consider the available routes to immigrate to Canada. We booked an appointment with an immigration lawyer in Tehran.

There were few ways we could immigrate. Investment was not an option since we did not have the funds needed, but there were two other options: The Federal Skilled Worker application; or applying to Quebec. We didn't have any idea about French, but that seemed to be a more promising path. I had enough working experience; an acceptable engineering degree and my wife had all the required qualifications. We committed to studying French since we had a great score for immigration through Quebec.

We started the four-year challenge to immigrate to Canada. We started our French courses from the scratch, and it took about three years before we were invited to the Canadian embassy in Damascus (Syria) for our interview in French. The Canadian embassy in Tehran did not have consular services.

In 2008 we travelled to Damascus. It was a calm city with nice people; a place I could never have imagined a few years later becoming the centre of one of the biggest conflicts in the world. We had a one-hour interview and were accepted to immigrate to Canada. That was the day all our hard work and long hours of study paid off. It was a big release from all the stress we had endured over three years, so we had one of the most amazing dinners that night. From that time, it took about a year to receive the request for medical documents and to take our passports back to Syria for the visa stamps.

On October 12, 2009, we entered Montreal, Quebec as immigrants.

Interestingly, I went back to Iran two months later. At the time, my wife planned to live in Canada full-time, but I had no intention whatsoever of doing so. I thought that business was booming in Iran, and I could go back and forth, maintaining my permanent residence card at the same time. I would work, earn good money, and send money to my wife to support her financially in the meantime.

I went back to Iran and vacationed in Canada for less than a month each time over the next three years. However, my first trip to Canada initiated some conflicts at work. People began spreading rumors about me, saying, "Sina will eventually move to Canada, and he needs to be replaced ASAP."

The difficulty started with my boss. In May 2010, my boss said, "Sina! This situation must stop. Either guarantee that you close the file for Canada or resign from your job."

It was a tough situation. I had to choose between the high income and lifestyle I had or a life in Canada. I chose a third way, resigning and starting my own business.

So, I packed and quit.

Within a month I started my own company in the oil and gas industry. The company grew very fast, and all my experiences and energy became great fuel for my new life as an entrepreneur. I had completely moved to Canada two and a half years later.

In 2011, the business in Iran started to face serious international economic sanctions and the oil and gas sector was the centre of it. Doing business internationally became more and more difficult. Chinese and Turkish companies were becoming the main players in the market. I always worked with western companies and the new culture was a bit unknown for me. Competing became challenging.

In December 2011, a few months after my wife's father passed away, she asked for a divorce after 10 years of marriage.

I was shocked to the core. In a million years, I would not have expected her to break this news to me. For all those years, I worked very long hours, thinking, "I am supporting my wife in Canada and that's what a responsible husband would do". I learned later that I should have paid more attention to what she truly needed: emotional support.

The divorce put a lot of stress on me for logistical reasons. To save my Canadian residency, I had to remain in Canada for a minimum two years. I also wanted to end my marriage in a civilized manner, so I had to sell my main residence in Tehran and split the money between myself and my wife.

The ever-worsening business in Iran, combined with the shocking divorce, prompted me to fly to Canada on October 14, 2012, with the intention of staying.

I arrived in Canada with $60,000 and rented a furnished basement and looked for opportunities. Back in 2010 I had registered a company in Ontario named Samia Canada as a potential partner for my company in Iran.

During the first few months, I traveled to Calgary, AB, the hub of the oil and gas industry in Canada, to evaluate potential job opportunities. Those years served as the peak of the oil and gas industry in Canada. I was offered two separate high salary jobs at the reputable companies, Husky and JP Morgan. Although the numbers seemed tempting, I didn't surrender this time. I told myself, "This is your chance to make your dream of having your own business come true. Don't give in to temptation."

So, I planned to focus on Samia Canada. I rented a shared office space in Toronto and began doing some marketing. Meanwhile I started traveling back and forth to China to find sources for a product (Honeycomb Panels). I had become familiar with a potential Australian partner. I didn't have the slightest idea how I could build a business around it, yet I knew the product was awesome and sensed that there could be fantastic business opportunities.

During one of my trips to China, I met a businessman with an Iranian background who made a significant impact on the future of my business.

He was living in Shanghai for almost 15 years and was experienced with the Chinese market. He was importing and exporting iron ore and cement. He told me that he had lots of connections in the oil and gas industry. Many of them were his customers and he could introduce us to them.

I checked him out and found that he was indeed a well-known and experienced businessman known by many big players in the Chinese oil and gas sector.

I spent $40,000 of my limited savings on the office and salaries alone, while I was waiting for the partner's investment to come in. In February 2014, we booked tickets to travel to China to make the final presentation to my partner and his legal and financial team. Two days prior to our flight I received a shocking phone call informing me that he was in the hospital. The meeting needed to be postponed. At first, I thought," OK, not a big deal. We'll just do it a week or two later." However, no news came my way in the following days. I followed up with his office and was not given a solid answer. I checked with others and discovered that he had been sent to jail for an undisclosed reason, with no release date.

My situation was critical. I had transferred most of the shares of Samia Canada into this man's name and he was now in jail. Meanwhile I had spent nearly $40,000 of my own money and found myself feeling lonely and financially strained. I thought to myself, "You have two options Sina. You can either declare yourself bankrupt, or you can close down the office, suck it up, and start from scratch once again." I soon discovered that bankruptcy was not an option. The only choice left to me was to make the difficult choice and shutdown the office.

I called my landlord the following day and let him know that I wanted to cancel my lease. I also gave notice to my staff that I was going to close the company at the end of the month. With only $10,000 in the bank and a partner in jail, I was in a very tough position. I believe the personal development I was doing at that time helped me navigate through that difficult time. I told myself, "You can make it right. You were the one who found the honeycomb panels in China in the first place. You were the one who made connections with all those international companies. You may have lost your partner, but you can succeed without him as well."

What made me worried at the time was that 70% of the shares of the company were still under my partner's name, and I feared he might have committed some serious crimes that might make me liable. So, I registered another company named Samicore, which focused solely on honeycomb panels. I quickly rented a small, shared office and a small warehouse space, and I started marketing and making some sales. It was around that time that my sister immigrated to Canada and started working with me as well.

Undoubtedly my ex-wife had the first and biggest impact on me. Our divorce pushed me to make the right decision of permanently moving to Canada. After that, my dad offered me his very limited savings to recover when I was completely hopeless.

One day in April 2015, the tenant who I had sublet the small warehouse space from announced that he was moving out and he was going to end his lease with the landlord. I was again faced with a difficult dilemma: continue struggling and move from this tiny space to another; or take the opportunity and jump to the next level. This meant renting the whole warehouse space for my own business.

The second option, scary as it was, felt intuitively right to me. I thought to myself, "If I play big and rent this whole space, I can reach out to big architectural firms, invite them to my showroom, showcase big samples of my products and eventually get much more business." Staying small wouldn't allow me to enter the big league.

I was negotiating a partnership with a huge fabrication plant in Montreal which could take my business to a whole new level, and I knew if I didn't go big, there was no chance of them partnering up with a small company like mine. Everything pointed to the fact that I would be better off to rent the whole space for myself, but the stakes were too high. The rent was $6,000, and my budget was very tight. I needed to decide, and I needed to make it fast.

That was the time that Reza, my friend, and Leila, his wife, noticed that I was anxious and stuck. They said, "Sina, we have a $15,000 line of credit that we don't need at present. You can use it toward the rent. We're in no rush for you to give the money back to us. Just pay the interest. Besides, we'll rent an office from you ourselves." I took the leap of faith and signed the lease agreement for the whole space.

I am very realistic about life in Canada. I experienced days where I was under a significant amount of pressure. However, what I learned and experienced in this country is that there is no limit to the type of life you can have.

I always worked hard in Iran; it was what I had

to do to be a success. What I was looking for and what I found was my freedom and respect. I saw the life I imagined in the magazine on my friend's coffee table.

Many things have changed since I arrived in Canada. When I started self-development skills in 2014, I stopped blaming others and circumstances for my personal failures. I found time to self-educate. I dared to criticize myself and as a result was able to analyze my past experiences and mistakes to prevent their repetition in future.

Canada, its values, and culture, encouraged me to think about community rather than focusing on myself. Contributing to the community is one of the most enjoyable gifts that I could find in Canada.

Many people give up quickly and those who are persistent will win. You must decide to prepare yourself and adjust your knowledge, culture, mindset, and lifestyle to live here.

"Canadians are patient, welcoming, and flexible, and immigrants should push themselves to contribute."

No matter which political party is governing Canada, humanity, responsibility, care, and support is in the soul of this country. Canada gave me the opportunity to have three successful businesses in only seven years with a small amount of money, a vision, and passion.

I married again happily and successfully, found amazing friends, and love every hour of the life I have. This is because of Canada, and I am thankful that I immigrated to this brilliant country.

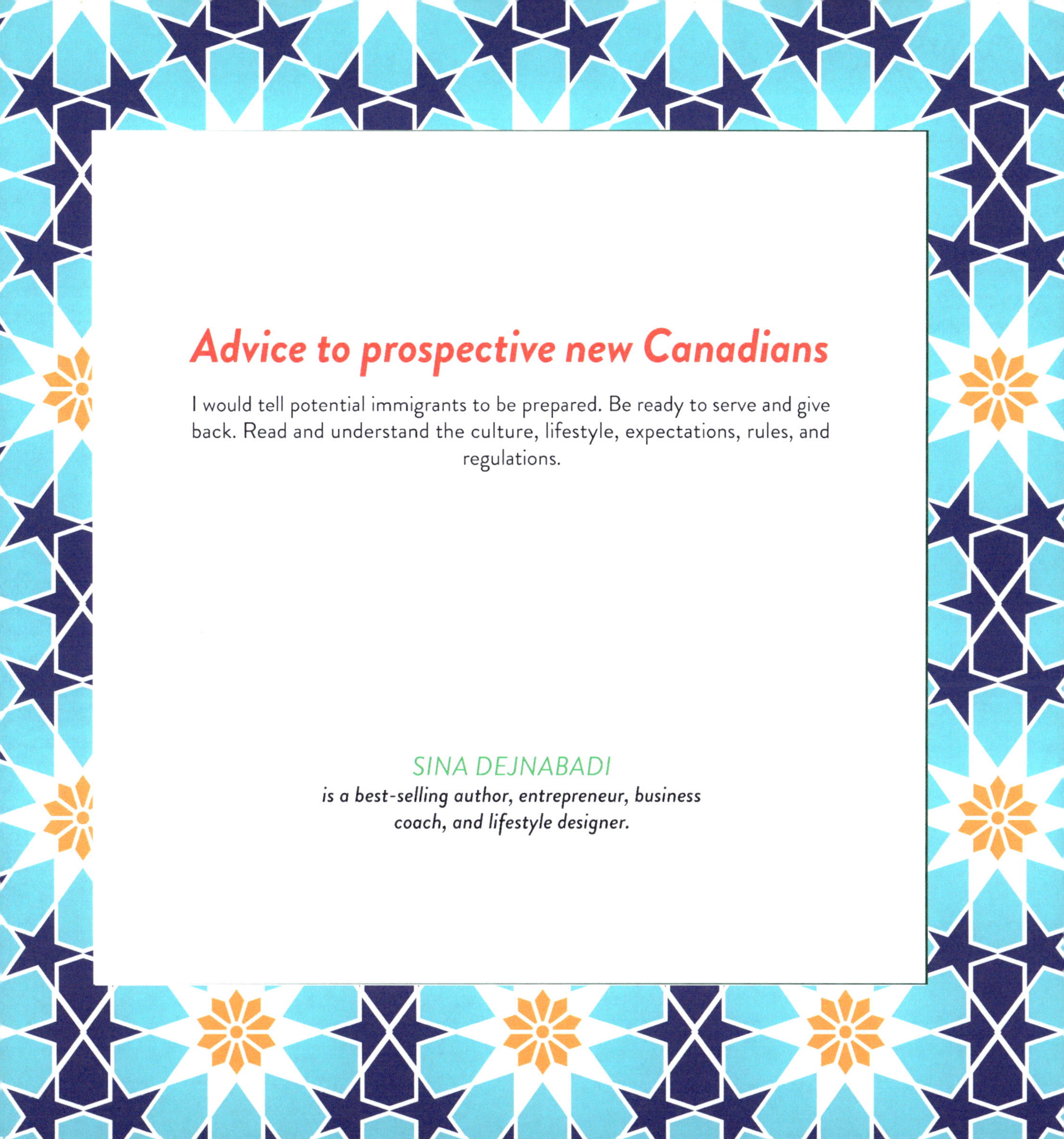

Advice to prospective new Canadians

I would tell potential immigrants to be prepared. Be ready to serve and give back. Read and understand the culture, lifestyle, expectations, rules, and regulations.

SINA DEJNABADI

is a best-selling author, entrepreneur, business coach, and lifestyle designer.

I Won The Lottery...Twice

Shula Tennenbaum

Israel

My real adult life began after my mandatory military service in Israel, and I met my first husband and became a mother at the very young age of 20. My marriage ended a year later in a messy and bitter divorce.

As I was a single mother working at a school as an administrative assistant, I took on another part time job at local pharmacy to make ends meet. That was where I met my second husband, Menachem, (the owner of the pharmacy), 20 years my senior. Shortly after starting our relationship, I learned that he was working towards immigrating to Canada as an investor. After months of research, networking, and trying to find the right location for a restaurant, he received the call that the perfect location was ready for him at First Canadian Place in Downtown Toronto. I was ecstatic to have an opportunity to start a new life.

Menachem and I had to be separated for a year while he came to Canada to establish the business. He promised that he would write me every single day and so he did. I received hundreds of letters from him describing the steps, process, hurdles, and sacrifices he had to make daily. He invested most of his money in this restaurant which left him no choice but to sleep on a couch in a friend's house and take public transportation.

"Canada allowed me to get back on my feet."

It was difficult to stay positive but was excited to reunite with Menachem to start our lives together in Canada.

I finally joined Menachem in Canada but had to leave my seven-year-old son behind for a year while settling in and concentrating on establishing a business. Once I had received my landed immigrant status, I knew that I wanted to make Canada my home with my sone. It was extremely hard to convince my parents to allow me to uproot my son and take him so far away from them. They had raised, protected, and sheltered him since he was born. After weeks of endless fighting, crying, and mixed emotions, I finally received the approval from my parents with a few conditions—that we live in a Jewish neighbourhood; that he attends a Jewish school; and that he come to visit at least once a year.

We became permanent residents in 1984.

My son adjusted well in Canada, so I began working at our restaurant all day and all night. We gave our heart and soul to this restaurant which was successful, and we subsequently opened another. I absolutely loved managing the restaurants. I loved the downtown vibe. It reminded me of the hustle and bustle of Israel only without the soldiers roaming around the city in every corner.

Our first five years in Canada totally revolved around the restaurants. While we built a successful business, I was mentally and physically exhausted. Within a few years we decided to sell the restaurants. While Menachem was semi-retired, I was given the opportunity to work at Associated Hebrew School as the main office secretary (not knowing that I would spend the next 25 years working there).

One day I received a call at work from Menachem to say that we won $40,000.00 in the lottery. I did not believe him and hung up the phone thinking this was a lame prank. To my surprise when I got home, he showed me that we did in fact win the lottery, but the figure was way off… it was over a million dollars. Most would think that our lives were set. Within a few years Menachem and I divorced. I was left with a second mortgage on our house, finding myself almost in the same financial position I had been initially before moving to Canada. I continued to work hard and supplemented my income by organizing and promoting Israeli singers to come to Canada and perform for the Jewish/Israeli community within the Greater Toronto Area. This was very rewarding. I became very popular within the community and was able to network and meet incredible individuals.

I have re-established my life and become financially independent. I do not believe that I could have done this if I had been living in a different country. Canada allowed me to get back on my feet. I consider Canada to be a very generous and welcoming country, providing lots of opportunities for success. I was able to give myself and my son a much higher standard of living.

Advice to prospective new Canadians

My advice for the residents of Canada and anybody working towards relocating is to appreciate what the country has to offer. Contribute to the community and bring all the skills and knowledge you must help the economy and enhance the culture and diversity.

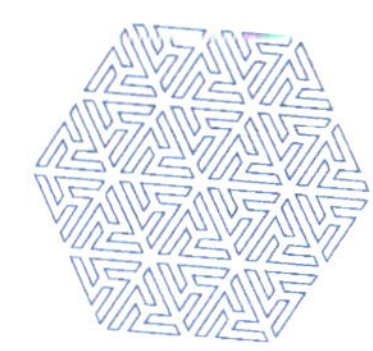

I Had No Choice... I Made the Best of It

Alex Scovino

Venezuela

I was born in Venezuela in 1963. I am the fourth of five siblings. My dad died in an earthquake when I was three years old, and my mom worked very hard to raise us just by herself. I grew up in a small city surrounded by mountains. When I finished high school, my mom told me she couldn't afford to pay for my university studies, so I applied for a scholarship at a local university and chose a career within its available options. Even though science wasn't my favorite field, I got a degree in industrial engineering. At the end of my studies, I was called to be part of a project to change the organizational culture of my university with the goal of improving efficiency and quality. The project was led by a consulting group whose members were mainly psychologists. That experience was a landmark in my life.

Once I got the degree, I found an engineering job in another city. I don't recall those as happy days. My work as an engineer was boring and empty. I couldn't find any joy working with machines and cold numbers. I managed to keep motivated by also studying organizational behaviour. I kept in contact with the consulting group and once I got my degree, they offered me a job.

Our work was advising companies about how to improve efficiencies and how to change behavioural patterns and organizational models. I worked with the employees by giving them a protagonist role in the changes. After two years, my colleagues convinced me to get a degree in psychology, which I did. I associated with a colleague and opened my own consulting company. I expanded my work to include marketing, business image, and strategic planning projects. I can say that we were very successful.

"We were forced to leave the country, abandoning our careers, family, and friends."

I worked very hard. I was married to a woman who was also an engineer and worked in the Venezuela office of a French oil company. We were not rich, but we lived in comfort, owning a nice home and being upper middle class.

During those years, I was involved in some minor political activism and my work as a business consultant was known and somehow recognized in the political field. In 1998, Hugo Chavez won the presidency of my country and soon we started to feel the effects of his leftist-Cuban Style ideas. In 2001, concerned for the future of the country, different sectors started a campaign aimed at forcing Chavez to either change his leftist policies or resign. I helped with the strategy and management of the image and the media of that campaign.

Politically, the campaign was a failure, and, in the aftermath, we were persecuted by Chavez's

"I came from a country with a culturally homogenous society, and I had to learn how to live in one that was multicultural."

government. We were forced to leave the country, abandoning our careers, family, and friends.

Canada was the only option we had because of their refugee program.

We came to Canada, applying as refuges. After about five years our application was refused. We appealed and were refused again. We were advised to apply for residency for humanitarian reasons and three years later we were approved. Our process to get permanent residency lasted eight to nine years.

My more than 15 years of work experience didn't count in Canada because all the open jobs were asking for "Canadian Experience". I couldn't practice as a psychologist because in Venezuela psychology is treated as a social science and in Canada it is considered a clinical science. To practice I needed to go back to university, which in Canada is very expensive. Luckily, I was able to use my engineering degree; my credentials were equivalent to that of a Bachelor of Engineering with a major in Industrial Engineering. However, that equivalency was useless due to my lack of "Canadian Experience". With a family to feed I had to accept cleaning and warehouse jobs at less than minimum wage. My first formal job was three years after my arrival in Canada loading and unloading containers in a warehouse. During the first 12 months we were one senior, two adults, and one toddler in a small bachelor apartment. We were using the food banks to get groceries and eat.

Once I started working, I gradually rose in the company, eventually becoming a supervisor.

The first shock after coming here was cultural. I came from a country with a culturally homogenous society, and I had to learn how to live in one that was multicultural.

The second challenge was realizing that multiculturalism was treated more as a marketing term rather than a real advantage. I found myself being discriminated against because of my accent or because I didn't study in Canada. If you spoke English without an accent and had a Canadian diploma, you would be accepted. If you had an accent (even if your English was good), you would always be a second option. If you didn't have a Canadian diploma, your knowledge would always be questioned.

Despite the issues, I find Canada to be a great country with many opportunities. In the social area, Canadian society really caters to equality and the defense of human rights. Adding to that, new generations are more open to REAL multiculturalism, and I perceive that Canada in the future will be even better in that aspect.

Life in Canada is safe. There is already a solid structure that supports social policies and protects the well-being of Canadians. That is something that does not exist in many countries. Of course, that has a cost, and it creates a high cost of living which adds financial stress.

Since coming to Canada, I have learned respect and acceptance for peoples' differences. This has made me more tolerant.

Like Bono says, the world needs more Canada. What is giving me even more hope is that new generations will bring even more to make Canada better.

Advice to prospective new Canadians

My one piece of advice is to open your mind. If you want a place that is safe, with equality and fairness, Canada is your place.

ALEX SCOVINO

is a Canadian-Venezuelan industrial engineer and digital artist living in Toronto, Ontario..

An Inspired Life

Charu Shankar

India

"I found grocery shopping to be a novel experience."

I grew up in New Delhi, the capital of India. Working in the United Nations and living with my parents in the heart of the city, I had a full life. My dad worked for the government of India as an advisor, and we were provided government quarters. Surrounded by lush gardens, my life was rather blissful. I enjoyed the cosmopolitan vibes that my work gave me and interactions with people of many backgrounds. I also enjoyed the culture and sounds and sights of this ancient city. My family believed in educating their children well and gave us music, dance, and language in addition to providing basic needs. As a result, I was encouraged to study French while in Delhi.

I didn't choose Canada. Canada chose me. Family friends had introduced me to someone living in Canada for a potential relationship. We met briefly, liked each other, and decided to get married. I never thought I would leave Delhi, or my friends and family. I had always wanted to stay in the same city, maybe even the same neighborhood as my parents. But Destiny chose otherwise. I left everything I knew to embark on my new adventure of settling into a new country with a new partner. Looking back, I can see how much courage this took; at the time however I didn't think about it too much and just plunged into being in the moment. I'm glad I didn't spend too much time thinking, If I had had a looking glass to see the future, I might have turned back!

I arrived in the suburb of Mississauga, Ontario in July 1995 after resigning from my job. During the first few months, I began to familiarize myself with a brand-new life, a completely new way of doing things. I had to get used to buses that opened automatically. I didn't attempt a bus ride for months for fear the doors would close while I was still getting on.

I found grocery shopping to be a novel experience. Not being used to fresh groceries wrapped in saran wrap or an indoor grocery store, every grocery trip made me feel like a kid in a candy store. The only stores I had known before were open air markets where vegetables were weighed by the vegetable seller. Prices were agreed upon through bargaining and usually a few extra herbs were thrown in for free.

Living in the Great White North was another new experience. I had to get used to the snow. I didn't know about black ice. After a few falls skidding on snow made me respect the stuff. I loved walking and so would just tie my shoelaces and head out everywhere, the library, bank, post office, grocery store. Sometimes I would walk and sometimes I would take the bus. Since I wasn't working and earning an income yet, I was mindful of spending, and would take a home-packed lunch if I planned a long day out.

Having worked at my dream job in the UN,

I expected to find work in my field quickly. What I didn't expect to find was a complete discounting of my work experience. An employment agency advised me to forget about my seven years of work and start from scratch. Following their advice, I plunged into finding work enthusiastically. Starting at ground zero, I accepted a temp job as a receptionist in a software company. My work was valued and within two months I was offered a permanent role. That eventually led me to accepting the position of an accounting assistant in the same organization.

I faced some challenges when I discovered that the universal human behavior of favoritism existed even in what I considered to be a place that was fair and just in its values. This was a difficult time in my professional life. I was new to the country and since I was still learning the ropes and fearful, I would lose my job, I agreed with the HR manager to take ownership of a mistake I had not made, even going so far as to sign a document agreeing to not share the truth with anyone.

It took me a while to recover from this experience, but I did move on to my next job of becoming a proctor at the DeVry Institute of Technology.

Along the way, I ended my abusive marriage, left the city where I arrived as a new bride, and walked out without a roof over my head and zero credit rating. Even through the toughest times of broken bones, I kept my spirit and never lost faith, ever. Soon I was able to collect a group of friends to sing in a classical music concert and raise funds to help build a special needs center in a small village school in southern India. On the outside it looked like I was helping the village kids. On the inside however, I received much in return. I was able to focus on something very inspiring to pull me through the dark phases of my life. I could see the light at the end of the tunnel. By turning my attention to this fundraiser, I was able to stop focusing on the negative aspects of what life had dealt me in my unhappy marriage.

Through a long process of self-examination, introspection, complete faith, and committed work, I managed to pull myself up and reverse my high cholesterol. I took a series of jobs, each one leading me closer and closer to my heart's calling of being a trainer. I also got certified to become a yoga teacher.

Eventually, I landed my dream job working at The SAS Institute. My journey feels almost like a dream. Now I coach others to land their dream job, to reverse diabetes, and become their optimum weight through yoga and proper nutrition. I help others become alive in, and truly successful at, navigating this journey of life.

Advice to prospective new Canadians

Here are some tips I would share with those seeking to settle in Canada:

- Stay optimistic. Try not to blame your new country or your newly made Canadian friends when things don't go the way you want.
- Reduce comparisons to your homeland. You are here now.
- Speak positively of where you came from and where you are now.
- Express gratitude for any opportunities people send your way.
- Take time to thank people by writing a note or taking them out for a coffee.
- Acknowledge help others generously give you.
- Volunteer your time.

CHARU SHANKAR

is a technical trainer and has helped coach thousands of users in technology. As a health and life coach, she also coaches people to land their dream job.

Best Decision of my Life

Alma Arzate

Mexico

I was an introverted child growing up. Connecting with people was a tool that I had not yet learned to master, so instead of playing outside with my sisters, Laura and Lorena, and their childhood friends, most of my time was spent by myself, reading. I remember the countless hours spent at the library after school, jumping from one fantastic world to the next. The library was a refuge, a place where I could escape the hardships of life.

I grew up in a relatively large city called Ciudad Juárez, Chihuahua, México. Like many others, we suffered through financial instability; however, my mom was a kindergarten teacher and my dad worked for the government, so a small yet stable stream of money was mostly present. My parents were hardworking individuals, who never failed to put food on our table. We had very few luxuries growing up. However, we did have our extended family close by. Some of my fondest memories as a child was going to watch whatever movie was playing in the cinema at that time, our pockets packed with homemade snacks. I will always remember the joy I felt, sitting beside my father, Rogelio, watching those stories come to life on the screen. He passed away in 2010, at the age of 68.

I was happy with the possibility of remaining in Mexico for the rest of my life. After all, who doesn't want to be surrounded by family, friends, and the most amazing food on the planet? That

"Our successful integration into the Canadian culture required extreme hard work and effort."

is of course, until I became a mother. In the mid-2000s, kidnappings and violence against women were becoming everyday occurrences in Ciudad Juárez. After many conversations with Jesus, my husband, we decided to explore options of leaving our home country to provide a better life for our young son, Jesus Eduardo. Coincidentally, around that time I received an email from a Canadian immigration firm offering me a free skill assessment to evaluate my eligibility to obtain a Federal Skilled Worker visa. By then, I had a master's degree in Business Administration and several years of work experience. I was a supply chain manager working for Johnson & Johnson in its medical devices sector. As the situation worsened, my husband and I made the decision to immigrate. After extensive research about its culture, values, and beliefs, it became quite apparent that our best option was Canada. When I worked at Emerson Electric, I reported to a manager who was Canadian. He was a good man, firm, but fair and kind, a real encapsulation of all the values and beliefs that Canadians hold dearest. Looking back, perhaps his character influenced my decision about moving to Canada.

Moving to a new city is always difficult but relocating to a new country is a completely different story. Thinking ahead about our move to Canada, not only did we have to move to a country with a drastically different weather and culture, but my husband and son would have to learn how to communicate in a language they had almost no experience with. Luckily, Canada has proven to be a generous and welcoming nation, diverse and accepting of immigrant skilled labor. All I wanted was for my children to be in a society that accepted them for who they were and knowing that Canada was a home for immigrants from all corners of the world eased my fears and made me feel a lot better about relocating.

The process of obtaining a permanent residence was costly, long, and complicated. We used the services of an immigration firm to attempt to manage the complexity of the process. The amount of paperwork that had to be dealt with seemed endless. There were many times that I had to cross the border to El Paso, Texas just so that I could mail a handful of documents that had been painstakingly translated from Spanish to English. During a critical stage of the process, I found myself having to fly to San Diego, California to take an IELTS English proficiency test. The test was not much of an issue as I had been speaking English for the better part of 15 years at that point, though I would be lying if I said that I was not nervous. Regardless, I scored in the 8.5 band out of 9.0. My husband was incredibly supportive throughout the four-year process, both emotionally and logistically, helping me with the gathering, submission and mailing of the myriad of documents. This journey would never have been possible without his unconditional support.

My immigration journey reached its climax when, from Mexico, I was able to land a job as a project manager with a Johnson & Johnson subsidiary in Montreal, Quebec, and moved to Canada in the winter of 2006, three and a half months before my family. Balancing a new job in a new country and culture, dealing with a harsh winter season in Montreal, and not having my family with me during those initial months was very challenging. To make things worse, the manager that had hired me and brought me to Canada was transferred to a different part of the business a few weeks after I started, so I had to get used to a new manager that did not know who I was or why I had been hired.

I managed to withstand those three and a half months until my family and I were finally reunited in Toronto, Ontario, where the company had decided to move its headquarters. I would describe our first year in Canada as overwhelming, challenging, and expensive with many surprises. However, as I would come to find out, not all surprises are bad. A few weeks after my family finally relocated to Canada,

I became pregnant with my third child! The conversation between me and my spouse went a lot smoother than the one between me and my manager. Nevertheless, I felt I had been blessed with a new job, a new house, a new country, and new baby on the way.

The challenges of integrating into Canadian society were very real, especially for my husband, who had to deal with a language barrier. Even the simple act of ordering a coffee was stressful for him because he was not comfortable with his English. My son, who is now 21, was ostracized at school when we first arrived because he could not communicate fluently in English. He is a very resilient guy, and soon mastered the language and made lots of friends. My daughter had a chronic hearing issue due to frequent ear infections, and she was behind on her verbal communication. We had her hearing tested, and thankfully, both ears were at 100%, but we still had to take her to speech therapy for about a year. All these challenges passed, and school and social integration became much better as we all developed new friendships.

In December of 2007, our third child, Gabriella Sophia, was born. Jesus and I now had a newborn, a seven-year-old (Jesus Eduardo) and a three-year old (Victoria Isabella). While I was on maternity leave in 2008, I was offered the chance to take on a complex system implementation project that three previous project managers had failed to accomplish. That also meant that I had to come back early to work after just four months of maternity leave. This was a great opportunity for me to return to work in a role I liked, report to the manager that had initially hired me and brought me to Canada and show her what I was capable of. I negotiated a flexible work schedule and worked three days per week for the first three months. Although difficult, this huge sacrifice of being away from my baby reaped rewards later in my career. I was promoted to senior manager of supply planning for Johnson & Johnson in 2011.

"The cost of living in Canada is high."

The price of our first house was ten times more than another home we had owned in Mexico. We were forced to sell all our assets in Mexico to just afford the down payment of a new house in Canada. The cost of getting used to new norms and rules was also high. For example, although my husband and I had driver's licenses and clean driving records back in Mexico, we were forced to relearn the rules of driving to qualify for our driver's licenses here. It took me a while to get accustomed to not looking over my shoulder like I did in Mexico. Canada is a safe country and safety is the number one concern I have for me and my family. Over time, we found local Mexican food, hairdressers, and made many good friends that we spent a lot of time with, which made our situation much more bearable.

Our successful integration into the Canadian culture required extreme hard work and effort. My husband has been the stabilizing force in the family. In the early days, we decided that he was going to stay at home, while I tried to make progress and develop my career at work. Without his support and love, we would not have been able to be successful and thrive in Canada. He is my rock.

We absolutely miss friends and family in Mexico. We miss the culture, the food, and our way of life. We also know that we made the correct decision to move to Canada. We try to compensate by surrounding ourselves with good friends, celebrations, and Mexican food, as well as ensuring that our kids learn about, and are respectful of, our traditions, while building new traditions together.

Advice to prospective new Canadians

My advice to anybody looking to move to Canada is: Do it and do it now. Canada welcomes new talent and internationally trained professionals are needed to contribute to our economy. Once you arrive in Canada, take advantage of the many resources available to you. Seek mentors within the community that can help give your insight into the Canadian workplace and culture. Maintain a positive attitude. Become your biggest cheerleader and your strongest advocate. Work on your brand every day and be known as someone that can always be relied upon. Most importantly, believe in yourself and your capabilities; otherwise, it will be difficult for others to do so. A change of this magnitude requires hard work, sacrifice, perseverance, and commitment, but it is definitively worth it. Best of luck to you all!

ALMA ARZATE

is a global supply chain and operations leader with over two decades of global experience across a number of industries. Alma has been recognized as one of the top 100 Most Influential Women in Canadian Supply Chain by Supply Chain Canada.

Burn Your Ships

Hashim Chaudry

Pakistan

I came from a privileged middle-class family in Pakistan, went to a prestigious private school and enjoyed a very comfortable life. In 2003, my parents made the decision to immigrate to Canada. I was 15. As a teenager this seemed like a wonderful adventure.

I soon realized that my privileged life in Pakistan was a thing of the past. No personal drivers and no servants. I had to deal with being an outsider. This was not the life I had left behind.

A few years after arriving in Canada, my father took ill suddenly. We were all accustomed to my father taking care of everything for us and now everything was changing. This placed enormous pressure on our family, and I had to do my fair share.

School was challenging as English was not my first language. In addition to school, I also had to work 40 hours per week to help my family. I started working at a restaurant and stayed in that job for 13 years. My work took its toll on my studies, and I dropped out of university in my second year. My family and financial responsibilities increased as my father's health deteriorated.

My earlier struggles and adversity motivated me and made me resilient. My work at the restaurant taught me the value of hard work and commitment to the task at hand.

When I connect with family and friends in Pakistan, I paint a realistic view of Canada. I do not paint Canada as a bed of roses, nor do I malign my new home. I speak about Canadian values, peace, and humility. I also speak about hard work, tolerance, and taking responsibility for your own successes. Labour is expensive and you must get used to doing the work yourself. Nothing is given to you on a platter. Racism is a reality, but do not allow it to come in the way of your dreams.

"When I connect with family and friends, I speak about Canadian values, peace, and humility."

Advice to prospective new Canadians

My advice for prospective immigrants is to burn your ships when you come to Canada. Do not be tempted to go back to your home country when difficult times arise. Canada is a beautiful country and probably the best place to raise a family. There will be many difficult days, months, and even years. Do not be tempted to go back until you have given it your full focus and effort.

HASHIM CHAUDRY
is a managing partner at an accounting firm and lives with his family in Paris, Ontario.

I was Not Planning to Stay

Shiraz Suleman

South Africa

More than money or status, I have seen peace and contentment as measures of my success. Growing up in South Africa during apartheid meant that neither peace nor contentment were attainable. Life in South Africa was fast-paced, fluid, uncertain, and unsafe.

After I qualified as an obstetrician, I continued to help my mother in the family business on weekends and evenings, manage my career, and help bring up my five-month-old son. Life was incredibly busy!

I was becoming restless about building a life and a career in South Africa. There was so much uncertainty and violence as the country transitioned to a new democracy. My focus was my family and career, and I knew that South Africa was not the place to have a peaceful and safe life. I began to seek new opportunities globally.

I found a short-term opportunity to work in Saskatchewan, Canada for four months without having to write any qualifying exams. I had heard positive reviews from my colleagues about working in this cold and remote community and I decided to pursue this temporary role. The timing was perfect. I was seeking new challenges and wanted to increase my knowledge. The process of working in Canada was not complicated for me. I was given preference because I was going to work in a community that was considered under-resourced and needed medical support. Even though I had no intention to stay long term, I applied for my PR card and the waiting period was a mere four months only.

"I loved to play and watch cricket and I now had to learn about hockey, baseball, and curling."

The first year in Canada was challenging for me and my family. I was newly married with a five-month-old child and my wife, Ayesha, was having difficulty adjusting to her new environment. Halal food became a challenge, and everything seemed foreign. Ayesha missed her family, friends, and social life in South Africa. Keeping connected with family via phone was expensive. I remember paying $1 per minute to make an international call. For me, the national healthcare was difficult to navigate, and it took a while before I became comfortable working in a new health system. Living in Canada was challenging for Ayesha, and she went back home for nine months as I prepared for my specialist exams. Adjusting to a new social, economic, and cultural environment made life complex. I loved to play and watch cricket and I now had to learn about hockey, baseball, and curling.

Did I make the correct decision to stay permanently in Canada?

Things began to change after a few years. Ayesha and I had two more children together, we had purchased a home and I passed my specialist exams. Even though I enjoyed living in Saskatchewan, we made the decision to relocate to Ontario. Our lives were evolving, and we became comfortable in our new environment. Our social circle increased, the kids were adjusting to school, and I opened my medical practice.

The first five years in Canada are very difficult and you must persevere. It is usually during this transitional period when most new immigrants go back to their home countries.

My patients became my greatest source of inspiration. I learned so much from them. I was given an opportunity to meet people from different parts of the world and learn about their culture, anxieties, and fears. No matter where we all come from, we all desire the same things—peace, happiness, and the best for our children. I never take my interaction with my patients for granted. Only Canada offered me the privilege to experience this mosaic of differences.

If you have an open mind, then you can use the differences to enrich your life like no other experience can. This is a very special thing.

My friends and family are intrigued about life in Canada. I tell them that Canada is an amazing country with lots of opportunities if you put your mind to it. There is relative freedom and very little crime. People from all over are welcomed and celebrated. People who are oppressed or persecuted can only dream of opportunities like this. I warn them about the cold weather and difficulties with adjustment. Eventually you do settle, and life does become easier as you build your network of friends

I have developed a newfound respect for people of other faiths and within my own faith.

Once you meet and interact with people from different cultures, religions, and beliefs, you develop a new sense of respect that you can only understand when you get to know people better. Apartheid did not afford me this opportunity. You learn to be more tolerant and understanding.

"If you have an open mind, then you can use the differences to enrich your life like no other experience can. This is a very special thing. "

Advice to prospective new Canadians

The adjustment phase is two to five years, and you can only take it one step at a time. Finding suitable work may be challenging. If possible, try to secure a job before you arrive. The cold weather will shock you at first and then you will learn to enjoy it.

SHIRAZ SULEMAN

is is an obstetrician and lives with his family in Toronto, Ontario.

I Came to Canada by Chance

Tawfic Mumuni Amandi

Ghana

Alone and living in fear, I knew I needed to leave Ghana. As an eight-year-old growing up in Ghana, my life took a drastic turn when my mother passed away. With no one to care for me, I was forced to leave home and live with my biological father, a man who I barely knew. We built a new life together, and my father went from being a stranger to becoming to my closest friend and confidant. However, just as my life regained a sense of stability and comfort, my father was murdered in the crossfire of a violent ethnic conflict between my father's tribe, Mamprusi, and a rival tribe, Kusasi. My world fell out from underneath me. In that moment, my life changed forever. At the age of fifteen I went into hiding to protect myself from the escalating violence that followed the public execution of my father. I knew I would be killed at the hands of the Kusasi if I was found. With no family left to turn to, a close friend of my father hid me in his home. During this time, I was restricted from going outside or interacting with anybody at risk of being discovered. It was during my time in hiding that my thirst for justice was ignited, knowing full well that my father's murderers would never be held accountable for their crimes.

Determined to protect me from the same fate as my father, my family friend obtained a falsified passport for me and purchased a ticket to Canada. Why Canada? I cannot explain. I believe the idea was just to get me out of Ghana

"Systemic racism is one of the major issues that impacts visible minorities in the workplace."

at all costs because my life was at risk. You could say then I came to Canada by chance.

My interaction with my immigration lawyer gave me a profound and different perspective of the immigration system. I felt that my age, 16, helped my immigration process to move smoothly. My application for immigration was prioritized by my immigration lawyers and case workers in my new, yet temporary, group home. Interacting with my immigration lawyer forced me to understand the profound importance of immigration and refugee laws and ignited my own interest in becoming a lawyer. I saw an opportunity to help others in a similar position and to advocate for those who lack the means to do so for themselves. I wanted to fight for an optimistic future for those who may have suffered deeply in the past.

My first 12 months in Canada were filled with uncertainty. I was homesick, and the culture shock did not help. I felt alienated from my surroundings. I stayed at Covenant House and was able to meet older immigrants who took me under their wing as a younger brother. Even though they protected me and sheltered me as much as they could, I felt lonely. This sense of loneliness continues to this day.

After completing my schooling, I enrolled in the Human Rights and Equity Studies program at York University. This program provided me with a foundation and context for a legal career focused on social justice. In addition to my schooling, I was elected as a senator and treasurer of the Student Council of Liberal Arts and Professional Studies, which advocates for over 27,000 students. This role taught me how to assist and advocate effectively for marginalized students at the university.

As an immigrant with no family or support structure in place, juggling school and financial pressures at the same time was incredibly challenging. I had to work as a security guard at night and then attend class during the day. Getting out of bed was a challenge but I never let my situation stop me from achieving my goals.

Reflecting on my life in Ghana, there were two people who had an impact on my life. One was my adopted father, and the other was my teacher from high school. Their influence, advice, and generosity allowed me to have a future. My heart longs for that same kind of mentorship and guidance in Canada.

Life in Canada is very different than what it was in Ghana. African tradition and culture are founded on community, family, and support. Canada, on the other hand, is focused on the individual. Most people in Canada are concerned about themselves and their immediate family. I yearn for the communal spirit that I experienced as a teenager in Ghana. Over time, my yearning for community forced me to centre my identity in my religion. I also began to normalize western culture. To fit in, I had to assimilate.

Canada does have its problems as well. Systemic racism is one of the major issues that impacts visible minorities in the workplace. Like our neighbours to the south, Canada has done a good job to hide systemic racism.

Advice to prospective new Canadians

My advice for new immigrants is to always remember where you came from and value the new opportunities in Canada. You need to train yourself to shut out the noise and focus on the future. Yes, you will experience some struggles and there will be days when you will want to give up. Remember why you are here. It is up to you to plan your legacy. Always remember to follow your path and never let the social construction or illusion distract you from achieving your greatness.

TAWFIC MUMUNI AMANDI

came to Canada as a refugee at age 16. He is currently studying to be a lawyer at the University of Ottawa Law School and plans to specialize in immigration and refugee law.

I was born French, but chose to become Canadian

Violaine Tourny

France

"The permanent residency process was long and very painful."

Three weeks after I got married, my husband decided to return to Canada. I was not given a choice and reluctantly left Sri Lanka with him. I took the first flight to Canada immediately after September 11, 2001, via Singapore.

I grew up near a water mill that was built during the 10th century in France. This beautiful area would later become the cradle of Christianity in Europe. My father was a doctor and spent lots of time in nature. He later became involved in politics. My mom was extremely creative and remarried an artist who opened a new creative world for me. I left France when I was 25 and relocated to Colombo, Sri Lanka with my mother and stepfather, who had opened a textile business. Even though I was not an expat, I enjoyed the life of an expat and made many friends. During my time in Sri Lanka, I fell in love and got married. Prior to my marriage and prior to coming to Canada, I had a lovely home with dogs. I was designing furniture for people to export. I was blessed with lots of leisure time, travel time, and beautiful weather. My life was tranquil, and I was at peace.

The permanent residency process was long and very painful. The process took much longer than I had expected: I underestimated how many documents I had to compile, translate, and send by registered mail to the Canadian government. Unfortunately, I did not have any support or guidance to complete the paperwork or understand the process. It was a lonely experience. I was ecstatic when I received my permanent residence status within 12 months.

For some reason, I felt more Southeast Asian than I felt French or Canadian. I was comfortable being around people from Sri Lanka and India and found refuge in Chinatown to find food products. In my first five years I discovered Toronto by walking. I walked everywhere and discovered so much in this mosaic of ethnical villages, a dream for an avid traveler. I wanted to understand all aspects of Canadian life and in the process, I discovered myself. The one highlight in my early years was starting my yoga teacher training. This experience allowed me to find true help for my healing as I dealt with domestic abuse. Yoga allowed me to deal with my violent trauma and heal my soul.

Life in Canada was not the same as in Sri Lanka or France. As the water goes down the drain the opposite way in Asia versus here, all seemed to follow the same pattern. In Canada, I was swamped with new information, new learnings, and so much choice. I remember crying as I made the mundane decision to select between multiple flavours of Philadelphia Cream Cheese. Which flavour should I buy?

It took me five years before I started to invest in myself and get accustomed to living in North America. Adapting to a new way of life was my biggest challenge. I soon discovered the world of interpretation services, and this role was key for me becoming financially independent and building my self-esteem. I worked as an interpreter for the Toronto International Film Festival and with vulnerable refugees in hospitals. I was on the red carpet by night and dealing with the most vulnerable people by day.

I always say that I was born French but chose to become Canadian. I chose to become Canadian because of the Canadian values of respect for others and tolerance. As I discovered the history of Canada, I was saddened and distraught by the way that the First Nations people were treated.

Also, as a victim of domestic abuse, I realized how little support was available for its victims. Canada also has a long way to go with valuing the skills that immigrants bring into our country and should do more to protect the environment. If you do not like the cold, Canada is not for you. The winters are harsh, and SAD (seasonal affective disorder) is a real thing.

"I was swamped with new information, new learnings, and so much choice. I remember crying as I made the mundane decision to select between multiple flavours of Philadelphia Cream Cheese."

Advice to prospective new Canadians

I started to feel at home in Canada after 10 years. You can have a comfortable and convenient life in Canada with many opportunities. Your life can also be very lonely and isolated, and you can feel very alone surrounded by millions of people. Toronto is the world in one place and for someone who has traveled a great deal, I appreciate the tolerance for other cultures and religions. I am allowed to live freely and pursue my passion for yoga, which I have practiced for 20 years. Walking the spiritual path sets a strong foundation for me to thrive in my other passions, interpretation, and advocacy through art.

VIOLAINE TOURNY

is a compassionate humanist, a contemplative artist doing her best and adding her sand to tomorrow's beach, using her talents, participating to a human-need-centered world for all to thrive and play.

Canada Gave Me Independence

Anonymous

Bangladesh

"I moved to Canada primarily to provide a better future for my children."

I come from a relatively wealthy family in Dhaka, Bangladesh. I had a disciplined but comfortable childhood. I was married in 1994 into a family with a different mindset than mine. My family was very liberal, whereas my husband's family was very traditional, women had to take care of the household, while the husband provided financially. I was a successful student but married young, so I had to forego plenty of career opportunities. I was still a student while I was carrying my first child. I remember taking my final university exams soon after giving birth to my first son in 1996. A few days after that, my father passed away. It breaks my heart that due to the strict rules imposed on me by my mother-in-law, I was not able to go see my father, and he could not meet his grandchild. I was not fully able to grasp the joy of having a child due to grieving the death of my beloved father. My second son was born in 2002.

I was able to pursue a career as a teacher for elementary and high school kids. I did so continuously for eight years. Life in Bangladesh was very comfortable in many ways as I was near dear ones, family, and friends. However, in such a close-knit society, having friends is a double-edged sword. There was a lot of social pressure, and I felt my life was constantly under surveillance. Every marriage goes through hardships, but mine was made worse by a toxic environment. As well, my eldest faced problems in school and by the time I gave birth to my third child, this time a daughter, I knew it was time for a change. I did not want her to grow up in this environment and I hoped that I could still salvage the childhood of my two sons.

I moved to Canada primarily to provide a better future for my children. I was going through a very tough time in my marriage, and during this dark time I held out hope that the Canadian application process would come through. My husband had applied for us with blind hope in 2007 but we never thought it would work out. The timing could not have been better, and we decided that this could give our marriage another chance. The move to Canada turned out to be a major blessing for me, my marriage, my kids, and my family.

We had applied for permanent residency through an agency back in Bangladesh. The agency was run by a very kind woman, who formerly lived in Canada and was also working at the Canadian Consulate in Bangladesh. The entire process took three years to complete. During this entire time, the agency (its owner in particular) played an integral role. She was very informative and helped me with setting up life in Canada. This included booking tickets, selecting schools for my children, introducing me to my new neighbourhood, and showing me the routes to essential places like banks and grocery stores. She even wrote an itinerary for my first month here and introduced me to another Bangladeshi family who would help us after I landed in Canada.

My challenges began even before my plane took off for Canada. Having to travel with two young kids and a nine-month-old baby was extremely difficult. My husband only spent a day to help me move into my new place and left to go back to Bangladesh as he had other things to take care of. The neighbourhood I was living in was very rough. Going from the comfort of living in my home in Dhaka to moving into a basement apartment during the winter season in a completely new continent was a very big challenge for me. My eldest son, who was 14 years old at that time, was constantly bullied—not necessarily just in school but also on his way back home from school by other teenagers. He was too scared to leave the house. I had to ask my neighbour to watch the kids whenever I would have to go to the grocery store. At times, I had to take my daughter, who was a sickly child, to the emergency—and I had to always schedule someone to watch my other kids. The basement apartment we were living in was in a deplorable state and I moved to a much better accommodation.

My husband and I decided to buy a house in Richmond Hill. I worked as a lunch lady in the local high school, along with doing plenty of other voluntary work within the school which gave me valuable Canadian work experience and I was able to build my network. My husband came back to stay with us permanently in 2013. This enabled me to get an honours degree in Economics from a prominent university in Toronto. I worked during the day and went to university at night. I built my network around the university economics department which would go on to yield plenty of positive results for me in the future.

A lady who was my academic advisor in the economics department believed in me and my abilities. She encouraged me to go on to do my master's degree in Economics. She also gave me the opportunity to start a part-time job in the department. This opportunity completely changed my life. She introduced me to the leadership team of the economics department. She convinced the board to make my contractual role permanent, and because of her, I now have a full-time job as a student success coordinator. She resigned from the university a short time later, but she fought for me in a way no one has. She was truly one of a kind.

I am now an independent woman, who has her own income and can support myself and my family. Overall, I would say my personal development has been incredible. In the professional space, I have enjoyed a lot of success in the economics department, which my parents and family back home are very proud of.

I lacked confidence in myself because of my very difficult time in Bangladesh. In Canada I learned how to drive. I learned how to take care of my family and carry out all sorts of errands without the support of a male figure in the household. The challenges and hardship made me really zero in on and realize what I really wanted to achieve in my life. I set small goals and used the motivation to set long-term goals. I was able to become more focused and determined. The respect I received from my colleagues made me appreciate myself and it built my self-confidence which assisted me with shaping my life in Canada.

I am no longer dependent on anyone else and can take care of myself. This country has given me so much; a good education, great job, life safety, security, and an education for my kids.

Canada promotes diversity and inclusion. When I visited the U.S., I felt that I was racially profiled. Here, I don't see any of that. When I go to grocery stores, malls, banks, I don't feel uncomfortable at all.

"I am now an independent woman, who has her own income and can support myself and my family."

Advice to prospective new Canadians

I would tell people don't think. Just come! Do not be scared to start a new life. It is a land of opportunity, and you will be able to meet your goals. This country will create the platform for you to succeed.

The War Helped me to Achieve my Dreams

Drazenka Culjak

Bosnia & Herzegovina

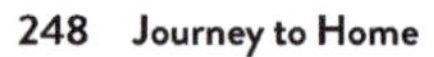

> ***" People were leaving the city, especially women with children."***

I was a double amputee survivor and was fortunate to leave Bosnia and Herzegovina at the onset of one of the most horrific wars of the late 20th century. Prior to the war, my life was great. I was working for one of the biggest aluminum factories in Mostar that had over 5,000 employees. In 1988 I gave birth to my son, Daniel. I lived with my parents and brother; my mom took care of my son while I worked. My sister Sima got married in 1989 to Mile, who was already living in Canada. She worked on getting her papers and permanently moving to Canada. Sima left in February 1990 and that same year in September, I went to visit with my sister and brother-in-law, and I fell in love with Canada. Being a single parent in my country was more difficult and not culturally accepted at the time. By moving to Canada, I knew that my son's life would be much better and there would be many more opportunities for him in Canada. While visiting, there was no way for me to stay or to get papers, at least I did not think that could happen. I stayed three months until my visitor's visa had expired.

The civil war erupted in the former Yugoslavia in 1992 and my sister and her husband were really worried about our safety and started the process of getting myself and my son to Canada. The war somehow actually helped me to achieve my dream of living in Canada as Canada was accepting immigrants who were in war-affected areas and had close relatives who could sponsor them. The city of Mostar was bombed daily, different areas would be hit sometimes randomly.

We had a basement with no windows and were able to hide there with our neighbours. People were leaving the city, especially women with children. My mom wanted me to leave with Daniel as well, but there was no gas in my car and gas stations were not operating. I was not able to walk long distances as I had prosthetic legs. Where would I go anyway? I was scared. I had no cash, and my money was tied up in a bank that I could not access.

The city was almost surrounded by military and there were only two roads out, but they were randomly bombed so it was dangerous to leave. One early morning we were told that we had to leave the house as the militia army was coming to kill everyone. My neighbour and her two children were hiding in our house and one of the kids was in a wheelchair. Since we were not able to walk far, we decided to stay with the kids and wait for our destiny. We were both sick to our stomachs.... literally speaking. A few hours later, we were told that it was just a military test to see how fast people could evacuate.

A week later the same neighbour sourced gas somewhere and came to my house and ordered me to get my son and my things and told me that we were going to Croatia to her cousin's house. My mother was crying and at the same time asking me to leave. She would stay behind and take care of the house and my brother, who was already in a uniform and going to the front.

So, my neighbour with her two daughters, and myself with my son, decided to take a more dangerous road and leave the city, praying quietly that our car would not get bombed, but at the same time hiding all our emotions so our kids could not see how scared we were. The road was uphill, and the small car was not moving fast enough to freedom, but we managed. We went to Croatia as refugees and stayed there for four months.

My sister called daily and was concerned about us and our parents and brother back in Mostar. As soon as the army moved, my mother came for a visit to see us in Croatia as she missed Daniel so much. When they saw each other they both cried and hugged and would not let go. I decided to go back to Mostar instead of my mother, to support my brother and take care of the house, as it would be very dangerous to leave the house unattended. To return was challenging, as the army was bombing the roads to the city. I saw so many cars that were burnt on the side of the road. I was scared but I kept on driving and praying that I would not get hit. As soon as I got to my driveway, the bombing started. I ran inside the house, so relieved to see my brother safe. I felt safe inside our house. I knew nothing would happen.

"The customs officer was shocked that we came with only two suitcases."

Soon after, the fighting moved further from the city, and my mother and my son returned.

At this time, I started the process of getting my papers ready for Canada. I had to do all the medical exams in Croatia and stayed at my cousin's house with Daniel as we finished all the paperwork. We had to go to Zagreb to the Canadian embassy for an interview and they insisted we both should come.

The fighting increased again between the Croats and Muslims in the city, but luckily, we got our landed immigrant papers at end of June 1993. My sister purchased the tickets for us to fly to Canada on July 7th, 1993. We had to pack fast. What to bring? I had a fully furnished apartment in Mostar. But there was no way to take any of the furniture. I packed our clothes and Daniel's baby albums. However, we needed a permit to leave the city. The city officials had gone, and no one knew when they are coming back. I found a Croatian military soldier through a friend who was willing to take us to the Croatian border through mountains where checkpoints would not be so strict.

I paid him to drive us in my car to Split, Croatia, and then drive it back to return to my brother. I was not sure if he would do that, but he did. Nothing was certain at the time. You could not trust anyone. The next day, we had a flight to Zagreb, then to Zurich. We stayed overnight in Zurich and flew to Toronto, Ontario.

I only had fifty dollars on me in case of an emergency. When we landed in Toronto, the customs officer asked me if I had a shipment arriving later as I was moving to Canada permanently. I said no, this was all we had. The customs officer was shocked that we came with only two suitcases.

We could not wait to see my sister and brother-in-law and be free again.

My sister promised me a job at the same company she worked for, The War Amps of Canada. My sister and her husband lived in Pickering, Ontario, on a nice little corner street. It was very quiet and peaceful. I started night school as soon as I arrived to learn English. Daniel was going to daycare. Every time a plane or helicopter flew overhead, Daniel would run scared into the basement. It took a while for him to realize that he was in a safe place. We both needed time to adjust to our new peaceful environment.

I was eager and anxious to start my new job at The War Amps. I did not need money as my sister and brother-in-law were taking care of us, but I wanted to be independent.

Finally, on August 30, 1993, I started my first job in Canada at The War Amps. The job was easy as I was stuffing envelopes with letters, but there was a huge language barrier. I hardly spoke English and whatever I knew at the time I struggled to say as I was so insecure that it would sound awful. I could not utter any words other than, "How are you"? and "Good Morning". My other struggle was that most of the people were immigrants, like me, with heavy accents, which I was not use to, so it made English even harder to understand.

I worked hard. I would finish 40 boxes a day, 100 letters in each, and other employees would accomplish maximum 27 or 28 boxes a day. The supervisors would ask how it was possible for me to be so fast. As I was not able to socialize with anyone, I just kept working. A months later my supervisor asked if I knew how to type and I quickly said, "yes". Once I realized what she had asked me it was too late to go back and explain to her that it was not true. I was worried about what would happen on Monday morning. I was too scared to tell my sister what had happened as I was worried about her reaction when she learned that I had lied about my abilities.

On Monday morning, I was taken to a big room with other women to start typing on a mainframe green screen. had a nice lady to teach me the process. She told me how to login with my user ID and password and started explaining the screens and what needed to be input on each. I could not understand a thing, I did not know what user ID and password meant. I said to her," You do, I do", meaning, do not waste any words on me as I have no clue what you are talking about. Just show me.

I typed as fast as I could and made sure I did everything correctly. I wanted to succeed so badly. I was promoted to the data entry department as I was the fastest typist.

This was when I fell in love with computers. I saw how much easier it was having data in a computer rather than on a paper. I was impressed and in awe. After a year or so I got tired of doing data entry, I felt like a robot doing the same work, day in and day out. I needed a more challenging job. My sister would tell me to be patient and that this was great job for me, but I was no longer happy.

The War Amps of Canada had a program in place that would give training to people with disabilities and give them a placement job at a different company for six months. The program was to learn computer operations or programing. I needed to do IQ testing at another facility for five days. If I passed, I would be given the green light to take the course. I applied. I believed I was hard worker and that I would be able to learn anything. My sister was worried that I would fail, lose my job, and must start all over again stuffing envelopes. I was determined to try.

I did great on the logic and math, but my English was not great. The psychologist was not keen on giving me the green the light to take the course, but I pleaded with her to let me go and she did. Thanks to her, my life changed forever.

I took a three-month course and learned how to operate IBM systems, printers, and tape drives. I also got my driver's license. I had to redo my written and driving test. I passed the written exam, but I failed my driving test twice. Mostly I drove too fast, it was hard for me to get rid of my bad driving habits from back home.

I wanted to move out and live on my own. However, I did not make enough money. I needed another source of income. My English was not good, and I had two prosthetic legs. My brother-in-law was a bouncer at a nightclub, and I asked if I could do something there. Coat check looked like an excellent job for me. I got a job there for two weeks and was fired right after, as the owners gave the job to their relatives.

A few months later I got a coat check job in a different club and worked this job for many years. Now I was able to afford a used car. Once I had a car, I wanted to move out. My brother-in-law convinced me that I should buy a house rather than rent. He told me to go to bank to get a $5,000 loan for furniture. I asked and I got it. I could not believe how easy it was. I had a lot to learn about my new country. This was exciting.

I was able to get my first apartment two years after I moved to Canada. This was the first time I lived on my own. I was scared and happy at the same time. My son could walk to school. We lived on the 12th floor and my son feared elevators. He learned how to lock and unlocked the apartment door by himself and wait for me. My mother came that summer to take care of him while I worked. I was not able to afford summer camps or daycare. Despite all the struggles, I was excited about my life and progress.

On April 30th, I got a job with big outsourcing company that had many banks and mutual funds companies as clients. It was a very fast-paced environment. I dedicated myself one hundred percent to learning and worked hard. I got an opportunity to work on a special project and after my six-month co-op, the company offered me a full-time job. I was on top of the world.

Beside my hard work I was lucky to have so many people in my life who supported and encouraged me through my career. My sister Sima and bother-in-law Mile. It seemed that everyone I met gave me a helping hand. I was lucky that I was able to meet so many wonderful people that could be there for me and support me.

I met friends who helped me with Daniel and would babysit for free. At work, I met people who would guide me and teach me new skills. With these skills I was able to pursue my career and be successful. I am very grateful to all of them.

"If I was able to succeed hardly speaking English, with no money in my pocket, only two suitcases, a small child and two prosthetic legs, anyone else can do the same."

Canada is truly a country full of opportunities. If I was able to succeed hardly speaking English, with no money in my pocket, only two suitcases, a small child and two prosthetic legs, anyone else can do the same. As always, I wanted more. I had this important job, but no real schooling. I needed to have real diploma. I wanted to go to college. I first took a college English course and gave up because it was too difficult. I went back next semester and signed up again. This time I was able to finish the course. For the next five years I completed all the courses and received my diploma at Seneca, with honours. I completed the entire program part-time, attending classes in the evening and on the weekends.

When Daniel was older, I wanted to take part in sports. Before coming to Canada, I competed in air rifle shooting, chess, and bowling. Even though I feared water and not a good swimmer, I wanted to try water sports. I tried rowing, then learned to kayak and became very good. I travelled across Canada with my club, trained with the Canadian team in Florida, and competed at the provincial and national levels for 10 years. In 2013, I qualified for the World Championships in Duisburg, Germany. This was an amazing experience. To represent Canada and to wear a Canadian uniform and flag was something I could only have dreamed about. I placed 8th. I was so thrilled with the experience. In the winter I tried sledge hockey but found that sport too rough for me. I had an opportunity to try cross-country skiing and liked it. I competed in cross-country skiing at the provincial and national levels for three years. I have drawer full of medals from cross-country skiing and kayaking. I also started training in the gym daily and this became my new passion.

One of the biggest highlights was the opportunity I had to carry the torch at the 2015 Pan American Games in Toronto.

"To represent Canada and to wear a Canadian uniform and flag was something I could only have dreamed about."

Advice to prospective new Canadians

I believe anyone with the right attitude can achieve anything in this country. I continue to challenge myself. It is important to give back. I have been volunteering in a hospital for over 20 years and I visit other people who lost their limbs and talk to them about opportunities and life with prosthetic legs. This country gives us so much and we need to give back. I am so proud to call myself Canadian. In the words of Amanda Gorman, "If we merge mercy with might and might with right, then love becomes our legacy".

DRAZENKA CULJAK

represented Canada in kayaking and cross-country skiing. She also carried the Canadian torch during the 2015 Pan American Games in Toronto.

An unexpected Commonality

Randy Pitawanakwat

As we have come to learn, there are certain similarities between the immigrant experience and the experience of Indigenous peoples. It is obviously ironic. We asked Randy Pitawanakwat to share his perspective regarding his life as a leader in that community. Specifically, we were curious regarding his feelings about alienation and acceptance. When reading his story, it may be useful to keep in mind the perspectives that were shared in the immigrant stories. The comparison is illuminating.

Aanii, Randy Pitawanakwat n'dizhnikaaz, Wiikwemkoong miinwaa Atikameksheng Anishnawbek ndoonjibaa. My name is Randy Pitawanakwat and I am from Wiikwemkoong Unceded Territory and Atikameksheng Anishnawbek. Much of my knowledge is a collective of understanding from oral tradition and experiences throughout my life back home in Wiikwemkoong and Atikameksheng Anishnawbek.

I grew up in a northern Ontario city where at times, it felt like I was not understood or valued as an Anishnaabe. I have only started to appreciate and understand who I am as Anishnaabe here on Turtle Island (Canada).

So many generations before me were not given that liberty; they were oppressed and forced to learn a foreign language and culture. When the settlers and colonizers came to Turtle Island we welcomed them onto our land. We taught them our traditions, how to survive, how to harvest and build structures that would stand up to the climate and conditions of the season changes, and taught them our language and culture. In return we wanted an understanding that a relationship between nations needed to be negotiated and renewed to ensure balance, which we called in our language Naaknigewin or in English; treaties.

Over time, this balance of treaty negotiation and renewal became one sided and after a while, the settlers refused to take part in these

"So many generations before me were not given that liberty; they were oppressed and forced to learn a foreign language and culture."

traditions and ceremonies. They pushed their agenda further and further. We are now at a time when everything is being brought to light and there can no longer be silence or ignorance of the true history. We must all learn the real truths and do something! I don't have any first-hand knowledge that immigrants can relate to this exact experience, however what I do know is that we share the history of colonization. Colonization is not something that is unique to Canada. From my understanding this occurred all over the world to different degrees. This is why I believe immigrants can relate to my story and understand my experience. We have come into a time when the term, decolonization is being recognized at institutions across this country and we need to act and 'decolonize' our own understanding of what changes need to occur so that we can have an equality. In that way our future generations can appreciate and pass these traditions on to their next generation.

In order to seek balance, we must stop learning from movies and documentaries written and filmed by White people, and dig deeper in order to find indigenous directors, film makers, play writes, scholars, bloggers, youtubers, tik tok creators, Facebook groups, twitter etc. We must look beyond what the mainstream media, and film is telling us to believe. The local news is not the definitive resource. For all of us to live together in harmony we should understand the teachings of the land. The land is our teacher and has shown my people how to survive for generations, long before the settler contact. In our teachings, we always start by recognizing the land as our first teacher and because of that, we offer thanks to the land for giving us the knowledge, the support, and the guidance to survive and continue our journey. This may have a different meaning to various people. Some would say that's thinking 'green' or 'environmental', but the Anishnaabe have always called it respecting the land or reciprocity with the land. If we are looking for reconciliation Canadians can start by reading and understanding what the term RCAP and TRC stands for and begin to add this kind of vocabulary to their everyday life. The question is "what are the calls to action that my family and I have implemented?"

I recall and Elder imploring people to learn about First Nation, Inuit, Métis history; "Ask 'Grandma Google" with a smile on her face. The reality is that too many of us know nothing about the true history here on what my people call 'Turtle Island'. In 2021 to not know where to start is like walking around without a phone or social media account. There is a wealth of information out there and you can start wherever you want. If it means, saying thank you in your language every morning to the land you're on, then that's good, or if you want to stand at the front lines and advocate for the rights of Indigenous peoples across this country then that's great too!

RANDY PITAWANAKWAT

is an Anishinaabe from the unceded territory of Wiikwemkoong and Atikameksheng Anishnawbek (Turtle Island). Randy has worked with the Indigenous community in the GTA for over 11 years and continues to advocate for the rights and protection of traditional ways of knowledge. Randy is currently a professor at Seneca College and works out of Odeyto, First Peoples' at Seneca, the Indigenous Centre at the college.

About the Authors

AZHAR LAHER

Azhar Laher is an educator, an author, and human capital consultant. He works with senior leaders on culture, inclusion, retention and becoming an employer of choice. His previous book, ***Confessions of a Dad: My Kids Don't Understand the Value of Money***, has received praise for highlighting the importance of financial literacy for young adults. Azhar is currently Professor of Human Resources at Seneca College in Toronto. His big loves are his family, paying it forward, and following Toronto sports teams.
You can learn more at ***www.azharlaher.com***

DAVID GARSON

David Garson has been practising immigration law for 29 years and is certified by the Law Society of Ontario as a Specialist in Immigration Law.David is a past Chair of the Canadian Bar Association—Ontario, Immigration and Citizenship Section. He is currently a member of the American Immigration Lawyers Association, a past Chair of the Canada Chapter of the American Immigration Lawyers Association and a past Chair of the Continuing Legal Education Committee of the Young Lawyers Division—Canadian Bar Association. He is ranked in Band 1 by Chambers and Partners legal rankings in immigration law.
You can learn more at ***www.garsonil.com***

Manufactured by Amazon.ca
Bolton, ON